Dr. Paul Swets is a counselor, teacher, pastor, and seminar leader. He holds a Doctor of Arts degree in English from the University of Michigan and has taught college courses in communication. He has had extensive experience as a speaker and family counselor. Dr. Swets is pastor of Christ Community Church and president of Personal Development Systems, Inc., a business firm involved in leadership and management training. He lives in Palm Springs, Florida with his wife, Janiece, and two children, Judson and Jessica.

Dr. Paul Stoop ... [illegible faded text, largely unreadable]
[several lines of heavily faded, illegible text]

PAUL W. SWETS

THE ART OF TALKING
SO THAT PEOPLE WILL LISTEN

Getting through to
Family, Friends, and Business Associates

Prentice-Hall, Inc., Englewood Cliffs, New Jersey 07632

Library of Congress Cataloging in Publication Data

Swets, Paul W.
      The art of talking so that people will listen.

      Includes index.
      1. Interpersonal communication.   I. Title.
BF637.C45S87   1983   158'.2   83-10951
ISBN 0-13-047845-8
ISBN 0-13-047837-7 (pbk.)

6   7   8   9   10

ISBN 0-13-047845-8

ISBN 0-13-047837-7 {PBK.}

Editorial/production supervision by Alberta Boddy
Manufacturing buyer: Edward J. Ellis
Cover design © 1983 by Jeannette Jacobs

To Janiece, my wife—
my best conversational partner

Contents

Foreword

I wish that I might have had access to this book as a young man starting out in life. In that case my proficiency in the art of communication would have been greatly enhanced. For *The Art of Talking So That People Will Listen* by Dr. Paul W. Swets is a masterpiece in the important skill of talking to people effectively and good personal relations. Indeed this book is one of the most complete and in-depth treatments of the subject that has come to my attention.

For a public speaker, or anyone who wants to communicate better, this book should be a must because one communicates through words, facial expression, gestures, body flow, and the intangible but powerful transmission of personality. Beyond that the speaker will either attract or set up resistance by the degree to which a subtle but real feeling of caring comes through to his audience.

Many years ago one of Hollywood's greatest character actors made a comeback from failure to success when he began "loving the people in his audiences." He told me that he could actually feel a deeper sense of rapport as he sincerely projected love.

He was utilizing a psychologically sound principle of communication in that by taking people to his heart he was reaching them better with his mind. When you send out love to a person, as that outflow reaches him it seems that understanding is stimulated. Hence the communication of thought attains a greater degree of exactness. Thoughts get across as intended and devoid of distortion because minds have become more completely attuned.

Communication of this high order is actually a scientific procedure and is, therefore, subject to formula or methodology. That is to say, there are definite laws and skills in communication that must be learned as in any science.

And surely to be able to communicate effectively not only with an audience, but one to one, goes far toward determining our own success in life. Therefore, a book that outlines procedures of communication with the completeness of Dr. Swets' study becomes a working manual that can be invaluable. And I do not know of a book that more comprehensibly covers the entire subject of communication. Moreover the author himself communicates in a clear and understandable manner.

Dr. Swets not only writes clearly about communication, he also communicates clearly. He knows how to write so people will understand, how to talk so people will listen.

It gives me pleasure to commend this book to your reading and study. I am sure that you will be helped thereby as I have been.

Norman Vincent Peale

Preface

Communication should be easy. We've been practicing it since birth. And practice makes perfect. Right? Wrong!

We have learned to put words together so they make sense. We know what most words mean. Yet we soon discover that not everyone understands the meaning we intended. In fact, our words sometimes drive people away from us, even when we really want our words to draw them close.

After twenty years of marriage, Debbie came to my office for counseling because she felt the only alternative to the progressive disintegration of her marriage was a divorce. Her problem, she said, was a total inability to communicate with her husband. Debbie's problem is not uncommon. Countless marriages, families, and businesses break up because people practice a form of communication that separates them from others instead of creating understanding and a sense of togetherness.

Person-to-person communication is a problem for so many of us because we actually have never been trained in the art of getting through to people. Vocabulary and grammar training provide us with only the artist's canvas and paint. That training is totally inadequate in showing us how to put the two together so that people will see the picture we want them to see. *The Art of Talking So That People Will Listen* fills that void in our training.

You and I can talk so that people will understand. And we can learn to listen so well that people will enjoy talking with us. The key is knowing exactly *what* we want to happen when we communicate and *how* to make it happen.

Setting clear communication goals helps us to make small yet significant adjustments in what we say and how we listen. Making the right adjustments at the right time truly is an art, but taken one step at a time that art is simple enough to be mastered by anyone. Each chapter in this book guides your steps by presenting a clear goal to work on. Self-assessment tests, practical strategies, and plans of action ensure that you know where you want to go and that you make progress toward your goal.

As you achieve success in reaching each communication goal, you will:

- Gain control of the complexities in the communication process.
- Know how to create intimacy with those you care about.
- Discover what builds communication barriers between people and what you can do to tear them down.
- Win the attention and cooperation of friends and business associates.
- Feel that you present yourself clearly and effectively in social situations.
- Experience success in reaching your personal and professional goals.

In this book, I present a particular point of view about communication and interpersonal relationships. I am convinced that intimidation and manipulation of people do not produce meaningful relationships. Any power or control gained by such techniques is eventually offset by the loss of honest and open communication. To experience a real winning effect, we need to move from egocentric tendencies toward patterns of understanding and cooperation in our talks with one another.

My viewpoint has evolved from my training in psychology, theology, and rhetoric, but it also has been tried and tested in my own experience. I know the agony of trying to get through to someone and failing. I also know the immeasurable joy of having a heart-to-heart talk and experiencing the pleasure not only of being understood, but also of understanding.

It was during such a heart-to-heart talk with my son that I asked, "Do you think we should pray that this book will be a best-seller?" He answered, "No, Dad. We should pray that it will help people." So let it be!

ACKNOWLEDGMENTS

I want to acknowledge my special indebtedness to the following:

- Richard Young, my rhetoric professor at the University of Michigan, who taught me so much about effective communication;
- Robert DeHaan and Robert Brown, my psychology professors at Hope College, who sparked my fascination about how people interact with one another and how children develop psychologically;
- David Myers, professor of psychology at Hope College, who offered excellent suggestions for the chapter on persuasion;
- Tod Bossert, clinical psychologist, who helped me develop the conflict resolution model in Chapter 10;
- Watson Duncan III, chairman of the Communications Department of Palm Beach Junior College, who encouraged me early on with his great enthusiasm for this project;
- George Froehlich, who read and corrected my manuscript more times than he can remember and provided positive support throughout the process;
- Blaise Levai, Kate Sampson, and Venila Van Voorthuyzen, who offered many helpful suggestions;
- Becky Robertson, Anna Koopmans, and Mary Vander Kamp, who cheerfully typed and retyped countless pages;
- Mary Kennan and Alberta Boddy, my editors at Prentice-Hall, who fortified my resolve through their belief in this endeavor;
- Janiece, Jud, and Jessica, who supplied more than enough love and creative diversion to cheer my writing on; and
- Norman Vincent Peale, who has demonstrated for me the persuasive power of enthusiasm, the practical power of a positive mental attitude, and the life-changing power of putting one's faith to work.

1

Play the communication game to win

You can if you think you can.[1]

NORMAN VINCENT PEALE

One of the greatest discoveries of our time is that an individual can control what he says and what he does by the way he thinks. Unfortunately, many people assume that they can't control the way they express themselves. Day after day they go on making the same conversational blunders. But the fact is that anyone can match wits against the "opponents" of successful communication and win. Assuming that you have the desire to win, the principle so aptly expressed by Dr. Peale applies to you: "You can if you think you can!"

To reach new heights of conversational effectiveness, you will need to set some clear goals that define what you want to achieve. Your mind then acts as a "steersman," guiding you with an awareness of the slight adjustments necessary to reach your goal. When NASA sent *Apollo 17* and its crew to the moon, slight adjustments were needed throughout the flight in order to keep the rocket on track and enable it to reach its goal. If these adjustments had not been made at precisely the right time, the rocket would have strayed millions of miles from its target. *Winning communica-*

tion is the result of making small, significant adjustments in what you say and in how you say it in order to reach your goal.

THE ECSTASY OF WINNING

Communication that wins a positive response from others can provide you with a new way of life. Nothing is more essential to success in any area of your life than the ability to communicate well. Nothing can compare to the joy of communicating love, of being heard and understood completely, of discovering some profound insight from another's mind, or of transmitting your own thoughts to a rapt audience. Self-concepts are enhanced, attitudes broadened, beliefs deepened, perspectives clarified, hopes restored, frustrations dissolved, hurt feelings healed. This is what Reuel Howe calls "the miracle of dialogue." Therapists have seen such miracles occur in the midst of their counseling. Perhaps you too have experienced such miracles when your own communication has been successful. And when you play the communication game to win, a big part of the payoff is that your partner in communication wins, too!

THE AGONY OF DEFEAT

Our communication is not always successful. When Pope John Paul II visited the United States in 1979, it was rumored that a news reporter rushed up to him and asked what he thought of the go-go girls in New York. Having been warned by an aide that some journalists might distort his words, the pope hesitated, then asked cautiously, "Are there go-go girls in New York?" As the story goes, the next morning a front-page news article read, "The first question the pope asked upon his arrival here was 'Are there go-go girls in New York?' "

Whether the story was apocryphal or not, it does demonstrate that no one is free from being misunderstood—not even the pope. Miscommunication has caused nations to go to war, businesses to go bankrupt, families to break up. Although communication technology has enabled us to penetrate outer space and make of our world a global village, we have failed to penetrate adequately that inner space of the human mind and heart.

Instead of creating understanding and closeness, our words sometimes produce the very opposite effect of what we intended. We hurt another's feelings, provoke anger, and create psychological distance even when what we really desire are understanding, intimacy, and companionship. Instinctively we try to avoid these painful situations. We tend to "freeze up" in our conversations to prevent the recurrence of miscommunication. Topics of discussion become limited. Feelings are repressed or redressed to sound more attractive. But when true feelings are not expressed, the passions in our relationships die. Gradually even the quantity of conversation becomes less until in some cases there is only the agony of cold silence.

Somehow we must break this vicious cycle. We need a way to look objectively at our mistakes and learn from them.

INSTANT REPLAY

In the sports world, players and coaches study game films again and again to help them eliminate their weaknesses and capitalize on their strengths. The function of this book is similar to that of a game film or instant replay. It can help you to examine your conversations as objectively as possible and take a second look at what worked and what did not work. Through examined experience you can make the adjustments necessary to play the communication game and win.

THE PRINCIPLES OF THE GAME

Can we increase the number of times when thoughts are transferred from one to another freely and well? Can we isolate that which promotes communication and that which breaks it down? Can we change our attitudes, our choice of words, our very selves? Yes! Effective communication on a consistent basis is possible.

Three important principles in this book tell you why this is possible. First, *communication is a learned behavior.* If you have learned negative communication patterns, perhaps by default, you can also learn positive patterns, provided you know what a positive communication pattern is and how to develop it. Second, *you can make a significant difference in the quality of your interpersonal communication.* Although you cannot control how another person talks to you, you can control your own response to that person and greatly influence the results of your conversation. Third, *when you act on new insights, you achieve understanding.* The adage about learning is still relevant:

I hear—I forget.
I see—I remember.
I act—I understand.

Strategies are included in each chapter for putting your knowledge into action.

A word of caution: there simply is no such thing as instant success in communication. But if you commit yourself to the principles described in this book and apply the recommended strategies, you can expect positive results. You will begin to:

Examine your communication experiences more objectively, seeing strengths and weaknesses.

Listen with understanding.

Develop skills for solving communication problems instead of being immobilized by fear, anger, or hurt feelings.

Assert yourself, speaking your ideas and sharing your feelings with confidence.

Learn how to say no when you want to say no, and say yes when you want to say yes.

Establish mutual respect when talking with children.

Enjoy a new intimacy with family and friends.

Initiate meaningful conversation in social settings.

Persuade people to cooperate with you.

If while reading this book you sense occasional repetition, it is a good sign that you are assimilating the concepts well. Deliberate repetition is built into the structure of this book. Research shows that retention of concepts is significantly increased when the concepts are presented several times. "Progressive redundancy" allows the mind to apply a concept or strategy more accurately and in a greater number of situations.

SKILLS TO WORK ON

If we have difficulty understanding or being understood, it is likely we have ignored some part of the communication process. It is up to us, individually, to try to find the problem and correct it. This is not an easy thing to do.

The following self-evaluation can help you assess your particular areas of need and interest and provide you with a standard by which you can measure your progress. Circle the number that best represents the frequency of each item in your experience (1 = seldom, 2 = sometimes, 3 = often, and 4 = usually).

Self-Evaluation

1 2 3 4	1.	People understand my thoughts and feelings.
1 2 3 4	2.	When communication problems arise, I am determined to solve them.
1 2 3 4	3.	I know the major causes of communication breakdown.
1 2 3 4	4.	I demonstrate personality qualities to which people are attracted.
1 2 3 4	5.	In difficult situations, I consciously choose how I express myself.
1 2 3 4	6.	The tone of my voice and the words I say communicate precisely how I feel about my conversational partner.
1 2 3 4	7.	I am able to listen deeply to the feelings expressed by my spouse and friends.
1 2 3 4	8.	My friends tell me I am a good listener.
1 2 3 4	9.	I can tell whether a communication problem is basically caused by the one speaking, the message itself, or the listener to the message.
1 2 3 4	10.	I am able to analyze accurately the thoughts and feelings of the person talking to me.
1 2 3 4	11.	When I talk, people listen.
1 2 3 4	12.	People tell me I am a good conversationalist.
1 2 3 4	13.	I say no when I want to say no.
1 2 3 4	14.	I assert myself because I value my own opinions as well as the opinions of others.

1 2 3 4   15. I handle hassles with children effectively.

1 2 3 4   16. I talk with children the way I want them to talk with me.

1 2 3 4   17. I allow loved ones and friends to know me as I really am.

1 2 3 4   18. I am able to tell people close to me how much I really care about them.

1 2 3 4   19. When I experience a conflict with someone, I know how to resolve it.

1 2 3 4   20. I know what to say in tense situations.

1 2 3 4   21. I know how to gain the cooperation of others.

1 2 3 4   22. When I ask people to do something that I want them to do (within reason), they do it.

1 2 3 4   23. I enjoy the highest level of communication with family, friends, and business associates.

1 2 3 4   24. Because I know the value of successful communication, I look for ways to improve my communication skills.

Here is a scoring guide to help you with your self-evaluation. Find your score by adding each of the numbers you circled; then check your total points with the following:

92-96 *Excellent.* You are undoubtedly a "peak" communicator. Give this book to a friend.

78-91 *Good.* You are well on your way. Focus your attention on the areas where you feel you need to refine your skills.

50-77 *Fair.* You are missing a significant amount of satisfaction which could be experienced through better communication. With concentrated work on the communication goals suggested in this book, you will achieve greater rapport with your family, friends, and business associates.

24-49 *Poor.* Relax! Perhaps you are setting your standards too high and see things worse than they are. By committing yourself to the goals and strategies in this book you will notice gradual improvement in your communication skills. Keep going. You are on your way to the top. You can do it!

Effective communicators are like good athletes: They work at it. A disposition is cultivated, fundamentals are learned, principles practiced, skills developed. Professionals know that no matter how talented they may be, they can improve their skills ... if they make the effort. But that, of course, raises the question for you: Is winning communication worth your effort?

Communication problems not only can be but *must* be solved. Since communication is the medium for every human activity—marriage, work, parenting, governing, diplomacy, you name it—the quality of our lives and perhaps even our future existence depend on communication that works.

When a friend learned that I was writing a book about communication, he exclaimed, "That's what I needed ten years ago!" We cannot undo the past. But we can make the best use of our present moments to understand another and make ourselves understood.

The purpose of this book is to coach you in playing the communication game ... and help you win!

ACTION STEPS FOR
WINNING SELF-DIRECTION

Each chapter concludes with Action Steps—brief guides to help you put the chapter's principles and strategies into practice and win the communication "game." To receive maximum benefit from this book, keep paper and pen handy to help you work your way toward your communication goals.

1. List the names of key people (family, friends, and business associates) with whom you would like to improve your communication.

2. Write a goal concerning your communication with one or more of the persons you listed. Begin this way: To improve my communication with _____, I will do the following: (list here specific steps you believe you need to take).

3. Think about the benefits you will gain from improved communication with the persons you named. Jot down as many of these benefits as possible. Let them motivate you to play the "game" to win. "You can if you think you can!"

2

Express
your best self

What lies behind us and what lies before us are tiny matters
compared to what lies within us.[1]

RALPH WALDO EMERSON

You are someone special! Of course, everyone has faults. But when you
choose to express your best self—that self that is open, humorous, interested in other people, willing to share thoughts and feelings, eager to learn,
able to listen deeply—when *that* person talks, people listen.

THE PERSON PEOPLE LISTEN TO

Those moments when you do express your best self prove that you *can*
talk so people listen. And they also show that if you want to improve the
quality of your communication, you must begin with yourself. Who you
are determines how you come across to people. Emerson said, "Who you
are stands over you . . . and thunders so I cannot hear what you say to the
contrary."[2] Who you are speaks louder than your words.

Attempts to improve the way you express yourself may make you
feel uneasy. As you compare your best moments in communication with
your worst, you may tend to blame yourself for not doing better. But

blaming yourself (or another person) is counterproductive. Discovering ways to improve yourself (and thus your communication) is to take the path that leads to satisfying relationships. In *I'm OK–You're OK*, Thomas Harris comments:

> It has been said that blaming your faults on your nature does not change the nature of your faults. Thus, "I'm like that" doesn't change anything. "I can be different" does.[3]

If we adopt the "I can be different" attitude, we put ourselves in a most favorable position to look at our communication problems and overcome them.

CAUSES OF COMMUNICATION BREAKDOWN

Our most troublesome problems in communication are personal; they are manufactured within us. It would be more comfortable to discuss external barriers to understanding (such as other people, time pressures, and frustrating situations), but it would not be more profitable. When we allow the internal causes of communication breakdown to go unnoticed, they produce persistent failure—failure to reach the top of our potential, failure to feel really good about our relationships, failure to bridge the psychological distance we sometimes feel between ourselves and another. To express our best selves, we need first to identify the real enemies of satisfying communication and then eliminate them. Our major adversaries can be identified as follows:

F - Fear
A - Assumptions
I - Insensitivity
L - Labeling
U - Uncertainty
R - Resentment
E - Egotism

1. Fear. Mark Twain may have spoken for many besides himself when he said, "I don't believe in ghosts, but I'm afraid of them!"[4] Even when we know our fears are not valid, we sometimes still allow them to isolate us from another person.

Certain fears are, in fact, necessary for survival, such as a fear of driving at an unsafe speed. But the fears we want to focus on here are those which prevent us from being our best selves and relating comfortably with other people. Here are some immobilizing fears many people wrestle with:

Fear of people, crowds, new situations

Fear of being judged negatively, of not measuring up to some arbitrary standard, of failing to meet someone's expectations

Fear of stuttering, saying the wrong word, mispronouncing a word

Fear of being laughed at if one's true feelings were known

Fear of not understanding someone and appearing stupid in his or her eyes

Fear of expressing emotion or not controlling emotion

Fear of holding a point of view on some matter that is contrary to another person's view

Where do all these fears come from? According to some psychologists, an infant is born with just two fears. "There are just two things which will call out a fear response," claimed the father of behaviorism, John B. Watson, "namely, a loud sound and loss of support."[5] All other fears are learned. They are not part of our original makeup and do not need to remain against our will. Unhealthy fears can be unlearned.

When we feel fear, communication is impaired. In order not to be misinterpreted, we say nothing. In order not to lose control of our emotions, we repress them. In order not to be criticized for an unpopular view, we constantly search for what others want to hear. As we deny ourselves, our world view is no longer enriched by variety but shrinks in upon us and imprisons us within its narrow confines.

2. Assumptions.   Assumptions can aid the mind in making sense of what we see and hear. Often they are correct. But they can cause communication breakdown when we trust them without questions.

To test the accuracy of your own assumptions, try to discover what the following figure signifies:

FIGURE 1-1.

Try looking at it from different viewpoints. Do you see a word with three letters? Are you assuming the letters are black or white? If you do not immediately see a word, it is likely because you are making a wrong assumption.* (See note at bottom of page for the answer.)

When we listen to someone talk, the brain is constantly making assumptions—hundreds of them. Each word, gesture, inflection, and tone of voice is interpreted, but not always as the speaker intended. We usually are not aware of the fact that we are selecting one meaning from a number of possibilities. The speaker also may take too much for granted. Speakers "assume they are being heard and understood," says Wendell Johnson, "when they are not, and so they do nothing to counteract the effects of the communicative failure and lapses, the blank moments and the misheard phrases, of which they are so innocently unaware."[6]

We often make unwarranted assumptions about the meaning of words. A study of the 500 most commonly used English words revealed a total of 14,070 dictionary definitions—more than 28 per word on the average. Take the word *run*, for example,

> He will give you a run for your money.
> Investments are best in the long run.
> Mike is a man on the run.
> Run along now.
> Sheila has a run in her stocking.
> The Expos just got a run.
> Do you have a run-down feeling?

Enough. We could run up a long list of variations, but the point is clear: Words can have many different nuances of meaning. One dictionary lists 87 distinct uses of the word *run*.

It is no wonder that as we listen to several words in a sentence and then many sentences, our minds misjudge some of the meanings intended by the speaker. If the listener assumes that the words he hears are to be understood only in the way that he interprets them, and if the speaker assumes that his words will be interpreted only in the way he intends them, then there is bound to be misunderstanding.

3. Insensitivity. Failure to accurately perceive the feelings of others is sometimes caused by an unwillingness to risk caring about some-

*The Word is FLY . . . in *white* letters, not black.

one. At other times it is the result of preoccupation, mentally existing in a different "world." A musician may be so engrossed in his music that he is insensitive to his own need for companionship. A mother may be so rushed to prepare dinner that she completely misses the significance of her child's question "Why doesn't anyone like me?" A husband may be so absorbed in a TV football game that he is oblivious to the frustration and anger of his wife. A president of a company may be so thrilled with a new marketing concept that he is completely unaware of serious problems related to the company's production capabilities. In each case, insensitivity results in miscommunication.

No one wants to be oversensitive. We need a certain amount of defensiveness and emotional insulation to cope with the normal attacks and demands of everyday life. Like a football player, we need some protection, but not so much that we can't make the best use of our potential. Insensitivity is *excessive* insulation. It is like closing one's eyes to the beauty of Yellowstone National Park, closing one's ears to a majestic piece of music, closing one's heart to knowing someone intimately.

4. Labeling.   Our minds are accustomed to distinguishing one thing from another. In the biblical story of creation, Adam's first task was to label the animals. Labels, like assumptions, are another attempt of the mind to create order out of chaos. We become experts at it.

But labeling another person can be disabling. The saying "Sticks and stones may break my bones, but names can never hurt me" is not true. Schoolchildren are notorious for labeling each other in uncomplimentary ways. In some families, in some workshops and offices, communication is marked by the putdown and subtle but vicious name-calling. Most people try to ignore the labels, but some labels hurt and seriously affect one's self-image. Some people waste enormous amounts of time trying to live down even innocent-sounding labels like "Crisco Kid," "Crazy Legs," and "Klutz."

Of course, words are not the same as the thing they signify. The name Susan is not the person Susan, but sometimes our minds fail to make such distinctions and we begin to act with indifference, sometimes meanness, toward those we have characterized by negative labels. If a father calls his son "Chicken Brain" often enough, the father may actually begin to act toward his son as if the son were not intelligent—and worse, the son might think of himself that way, too.

5. Uncertainty. Er, ah, well, maybe, I'm not sure, I guess so—these expressions are normal in conversation, but not *all* the time! True, certainty is not always a virtue. To claim certain knowledge of something not known or unreal is foolishness. But uncertainty can become a habit, a "safe" way of avoiding making a wrong decision by not making a decision at all.

Uncertain speech habits often come from fear, mental sluggishness, or the conviction that one is not capable of developing a valid point of view. If a parent or teacher constantly tells a child that his opinions are wrong or overreacts to them, the child may become fearful and cautious. Many adults are indecisive because they carry with them a childhood fear of making the wrong decision. Others are uncertain in their speech because they are not given encouragement for their views and ability to think.

In social and even intimate conversation, the uncertain person is often silent, tense, afraid. Under these circumstances, one cannot speak or listen effectively.

6. Resentment. Resentment is a bitterness of the soul that feeds upon itself. It looks for the worst in people and situations . . . and usually finds it. I know people—and perhaps you do, too—who have devoted their whole lives to getting back at someone, sometimes just anyone, to avenge some distant word of rebuke, some condition of life deemed unfair. They live their days pretty much alone and in misery because of the walls they have built between themselves and others. No one enjoys talking with one driven by resentment, for no one can be sure the venom won't be turned on him.

7. Egotism. Egotism conveys no true respect for another person, no genuine interest in hearing the other person out. Egotism creates serious barriers between people because the ego curves back upon itself rather than extending itself to another person. The listener feels that he is being used, that the speaker's words serve only an ulterior, selfish motive.

A surface analysis of such a person may suggest excessive self-love, but the cause might just as well be self-hate or a desperate attempt to achieve recognition from others. Sometimes one "egospeaks" as a means of reaching out to another and attracting his or her attention, completely unaware he is repelling the other.

No one likes to hear another person always talk about himself—no matter how interesting the talk may be. His words are not connections to other people, but reflections of himself. He looks into mirrors instead of building relationships.

Each of these seven problems is disturbingly *personal* in nature. But identifying the problems that cause failure in our own conversations is the first step toward building bridges of understanding and turning our communication failures into successes.

TURNING FAILURE INTO SUCCESS

Failure can be a stepping-stone to success if we learn from it; it can alert us to what we should avoid and point us in the direction we ought to go. This is especially true in our conversations because the means for turning communication failure into success are most often the qualities within us. Certainly our conversational partner is an important factor in successful communication. But Aristotle learned long ago that nothing is more important in communicating with another person than the personality of the speaker. Communication failure can be turned into success by developing within ourselves the following personal success qualities:

S - Self-awareness
U - Understanding
C - Care for others
C - Control of emotions
E - Esteem of one's self
S - Self-confidence
S - Sharing of one's self

1. Self-Awareness. The oracle at Delphi summarized a great deal of wisdom in two words: "Know thyself." Unfortunately, the oracle didn't tell us how. Through the ages people have tried to discover themselves by external sources—from palm readers to psychoanalysts. The most helpful sources served as mirrors or sounding boards, reflecting the self to the speaker as he expressed himself. Good friends are like that. Someone said, "A friend is one before whom I can be myself."

Another reflecting mirror is within you. You can cultivate self-awareness by persistently asking yourself what you really think about an issue and why you hold that view. Practice can help you to feel more comfortable with your views. It will lead to greater openness to new information and the ability to store it for later recall. You will begin to sense: "This is who I am. This is what I think. These are my values and my beliefs. Since I have thought them through, I am convinced of their importance and am comfortable with them. I know that I do not know everything and that not everyone will agree with me. But I am learning something each day and I have ideas, attitudes, and beliefs that are worth sharing."

2. Understanding. One of my favorite stories is about a professor who tried to impress upon his students the damaging effects of alcohol consumption. To dramatize his message, he placed one worm in a glass of water and another in a glass of gin. He showed the class how the water had no detrimental effect on the worm, but that the worm in the glass of gin promptly died and all but dissolved. "Now," he asked, "what does that prove to you?" Someone from the back retorted, "If you drink alcohol, you won't have worms!"

Of course, some people will intentionally misinterpret what is said. But when real understanding is desired, feedback is essential. By repeating what we think we heard and by asking for clarification, we are able to correct our misinterpretations and avoid wrong assumptions. Simply developing the skill of feedback could save us from hundreds, perhaps thousands, of pointless arguments, emotional explosions, and communication breakdowns.

3. Care for Others. When an audience senses that a speaker does not really care about them, they stop listening. But when it is clear that the speaker can empathize with how they feel, then even though he may be inept at speaking, he will get a hearing. The same is true in person-to-person communication.

People seem to have an uncanny ability for detecting how you really feel about them. They pick up clues not only from your word selection, but from your actions, your facial expressions, your tone of voice. Yet it is possible to so disguise your real feelings behind tones of harshness or frowns that others misunderstand and react negatively to you. I know a kindhearted old gentleman who really loves children but scares them away because his face seems etched in permanent lines of sadness and anger. I have seen a person try to convey interest in other people, but at the same time drive them away with shrill laughter.

Check yourself occasionally in the mirror to see if you are conveying yourself as you intend. Listen to the sound of your voice. Sort out in your mind the surface frustrations you might have with someone's behavior and consider how you would feel for that person on his deathbed. Then let *that* feeling dominate. Give flowers to the living.

4. Control of Emotions. Some people think they have no more control over their emotions than a computer has over its programmer. They simply assume that emotions such as anger, frustration, depression, envy, resentment, and jealousy enter their minds, determine their thoughts, and dictate their conversations. They take the attitude that they are helpless against the power of their emotions. They listen to themselves say things they would never dream of saying in their "right mind." They watch relationships deteriorate around them. They are their own victims.

Perhaps your fuse is too short. Anger may have become a habit, a way of dealing with frustration. But do you realize that anger serves no positive goals and achieves no lasting benefits? Further, anger is not something that just happens to you, as if it were an external force over which you have no control. It may be a habit, but it is also a choice. Therefore anger and other emotions *can* be controlled. We must believe this before we can motivate ourselves to change.

5. Esteem of One's Self. Self-esteem is not egotism, but ego strength. The person in whom ego strength is at its height most easily forgets himself and concentrates on others. People like to talk to those who esteem themselves because such people are not uptight, resentful, or easily intimidated.

Low self-esteem is often the result of accepting someone else's standard for your personal worth. Their standard is often based on the superficial values of beauty, money, popularity, or athletic skills. But you can choose those standards that are right for you. You can, for example, choose to see yourself as the unique being you really are. You can accept the human dignity granted to you by your Creator and affirm the highest esteem of your closest friends.

One of the most important responsibilities of parents is to build a healthy self-esteem in their children. It requires communicating an attitude of acceptance to a child not on the basis of what he does, but who he is. John McKay, during his tenure as football coach at the University of Southern California, demonstrated this attitude after an exceptionally fine performance by his son, John Junior. Asked if he was proud of his son's accomplishments in football, Coach McKay answered:

> Yes, I'm pleased that John had a good season last year. He does a fine job and I *am* proud of him. But I would be just as proud if he had never played the game at all.[7]

6. Self-Confidence. Built on the bedrock of self-esteem is the superstructure of self-confidence—the art of trusting and relying upon one's inner resources in any situation. Self-confidence is the willingness to take risks because one knows he can face himself without contempt if he fails. Self-confidence is the courage to meet new situations and speak competently to strangers because there is an unfailing support system *within.*

In conversation, self-confidence enables one to speak his mind and listen fully to the thoughts of the other person. Unjust demands, extreme positions, judgmental attitudes—these are as contrary to self-confidence as night is to day. Not needing to project or protect a false image, the self-confident person is more open to viewpoints different from his own, more able to speak with sincerity and integrity.

Self-confidence, like self-esteem, is not built in a day. The building process begins with drawing a blueprint of who you are, who you want to be, and how you want to come across to people. Taken one step at a time, the construction of self-confidence is then relatively easy. Anyone can acquire more of it when he acts upon his own clear plan for development.

7. Sharing of One's Self. Most people talk about themselves, but few share their real selves. Some take pride in being "private persons." Others let themselves be dominated by immobilizing fear and habits of silence stemming from childhood. There are plenty of reasons why people are afraid to share their inner being. Charles Schulz depicts one of them. See Figure 2-1 (opposite).

Lucy shows why it is unwise to share one's innermost thoughts with some people. But if we *too quickly* assume that others cannot be trusted, we lose the benefits of self-discovery through dialogue. Swiss psychiatrist Paul Tournier claims:

> No one comes to know himself through introspection. . . . Rather, it is in dialogue, in his meeting with other persons. It is only by expressing his convictions to others that he becomes really conscious of them. He who would see himself clearly must open up to a confidant freely chosen and worthy of such trust. It may be a friend just as easily as a doctor; it may also be one's marital partner.[8]

FIGURE 2-1.

These success qualities of personality are more important than eloquence or intelligence in turning communication failure into success. Anyone can develop these qualities by setting each of them as a personal goal, by keeping these goals constantly in mind, and by pursuing them with determination and conviction.

ACTION STEPS
FOR WINNING SELF-DIRECTION

1. Problems solvers know that if they can accurately state the cause of a problem, they have taken a giant step toward solving it. After reviewing the second section in this chapter called "Causes of Communication Breakdown," list your own most troublesome problems in communication. Concentrate on problems you can do something about today.

2. Sometimes we express negative communication patterns of which we are not even aware (e.g., talking too much or sounding judgmental). To increase awareness, try tape-recording or writing down some of your conversations for one week. Keep notes on what you discover.

3. Since feedback is essential for mutual understanding, ask for it from a friend who will be honest with you in a helpful way. For example, ask: "What do you feel are some strengths and weaknesses in my communication patterns?" Listen to the answers carefully. Try not to be defensive. Remember that awareness of negative patterns is the first step toward solving them.

Eliminate negative communication habits

The human species is unique because it alone can create, recognize, and exercise options. . . . It is part of human uniqueness that we are endowed with the faculty of choice.[1]

NORMAN COUSINS

Habit enters into our conversations to a greater degree than most of us realize. We develop subconscious ways of expressing ourselves when we answer the telephone, discipline a child, react to problems, or express emotions. These and so many other common encounters become matters of habit.

When habits become a problem in communication, it is because we are not consciously aware of how we are being received by the other person. If a son tries to talk to his father about a personal problem, a dream, or even a routine event of the day, and the father continues reading the paper, giving occasional grunts as a response, he could very well be destroying a relationship with his son—by habit. A wife who talks to her husband the same way she talks to her children could be destroying the very intimacy she craves—by habit. The president of a company may want the respect of his employees, but can destroy it through a rigid repression of viewpoints—by habit.

Can we change? Can we choose the words we say and the tone of voice we use? Many people are not aware of their power to do either. Not knowing consciously what has caused their communication breakdowns, they often experience frustration, loneliness, and worst of all, a sense of hopelessness. But as long as we make the effort and take the time to choose what we say and how we say it, even long-standing negative communication habits can be changed.

Computer programmers use the expression GIGO for "Garbage in, garbage out," meaning what you get out of the computer is only as good as what you program into it. If your communication patterns are not what you really want, you can *deprogram* your mind and start over with a program designed to produce winning results. "Programming" winning communication is possible because you are able to control four major factors that influence your own communication:

Your words
Your goals
Your strategies
Your commitments

CHOOSE YOUR WORDS

First, you can choose the *words* you say. From hundreds of thought fragments and sense impressions, you choose an idea and words to express that idea. These choices might be subliminal and habitual. But they can be brought into consciousness simply by focusing on them.

Here is an example of how one's choice of words can affect a conversation:

TELEPHONE CONVERSATION

Dick: Hello, Jane. I tried to call you for the last hour but there was no answer.

Choice 1	*Choice 2*
Jane: Honey, I've been shopping. What's on your mind?	*Jane:* Checking on me again! Why don't you stop doing this?
Dick: The boss just gave me two tickets to the theater. I want to know if your schedule is clear for tonight and if you would like to go.	*Dick:* No! I wasn't checking on you! Why are you so defensive?
Jane: I'm available and I'd love to go! What time?	*Jane:* Well, OK. What do you want? *Dick:* Skip it!

Choice 1 is straightforward, "easy" communication without prejudging what the other person is saying. Choice 2 ends in anger and a judgmental tone. But whatever motivated the responses in columns 1 and 2, it is apparent that the words we choose can make a significant difference in the response of our partner.

SET YOUR GOALS

Second, you can set *goals* which give direction and purpose to your communication. Without goals, your choice of ideas, words, tone of voice, volume, and body language is left to habit or the impulse of the moment. But with clearly defined goals, your expressions have the best chance of staying on target.

Goal setting can be a powerful tool in helping you increase your communication skills—but it also can be frustrating if your goals are vague or unrealistic. Wendell Johnson, writing in *People in Quandaries*, coined the term "IFD Disease" to illustrate this problem. *I* stands for idealization, *F* for frustration, and D *for* demoralization. According to Johnson, when you set idealistic goals without specifying how they can be reached, you will experience frustration after frustration until you are demoralized and give up.

To cure the IFD disease and to gain a sense of real achievement in your interpersonal relationships, make your conversational goals SMART. SMART is an acronym for goals characterized by the following descriptive terms:

Specific: Your goal must refer to an action which is distinct from other actions. For example, instead of saying, "I want to listen more when people talk to me," you can say, "I want to give my complete attention to my husband when he talks to me."

Measurable: Your goal must quantify the action or behavior you want. Instead of saying, "I want to listen more often to my husband," you can say, "I want to give my complete attention to my husband for at least fifteen minutes a day."

Affirmative: Your goal must state the positive actions that will lead you to your goal rather than state actions to avoid. For instance, rather than saying, "I don't want to feel uptight when my husband is around," you can add to your specific and measurable goal, "I will let my husband know that I care about him and enjoy being with him."

Realistic: If your goal is to be achievable, it must depend solely on your action. It is not realistic to set a goal that you can't control. So if you include in your goal that you want to initiate conversation with your husband by asking him questions and you do just that, you've met your goal, regardless of how he answers your questions. A realistic goal should challenge you to new action yet give you confidence that you can reach it with concentrated effort.

Time-Constricted: Your goal must specify a time framework for your action and a deadline for its completion. Instead of saying, "I want to start working on this goal sometime soon," say, "I will implement my goal tonight during dinner."

Putting it all together, you would write your SMART goal like this:

> I want to give my complete attention to my husband for at least fifteen minutes a day. I will let my husband know that I care about him and enjoy being with him. I will initiate the conversation tonight by asking questions during dinner.

A simple and helpful way of using SMART goals is to select one goal to work on for a week. When you have mastered it, move on to a second goal. Begin with a goal that you know you can reach with conscious effort and then reward yourself in some specific way when you achieve the goal. Let yourself enjoy the journey toward your goal as well as its achievement. Take pride in your progress toward winning communication.

PLAN YOUR STRATEGIES

In military terminology, *strategy* refers to the science and art of designing combat operations that will defeat the enemy. In communication, negative habits are like a wartime adversary. Deliberate plans or strategies are needed to expose and overcome that enemy. Your goal is to win the victory. Your strategy tells you how.

Specialists in behavioral change have found the following strategies to be consistently effective. To illustrate how they could be applied to your own goals, let's set up this hypothetical situation. You and your spouse don't communicate well. Little obstacles become big barriers. To fill in the painful silence, you talk. But your spouse then complains that you don't really listen. So you set this goal:

> Prior to bedtime tonight, I will ask questions of and listen attentively to my spouse for a period of at least fifteen minutes.

Then you work on the following strategies:

Define Your Obstacles.   Unless you know what your obstacles are, you will not know how to break through them or go around them. List several obstacles on paper, grouping those that are similar. Then number each item or group of items according to its priority or importance to you so you will know what to deal with first.

Here are some possible obstacles related to the above goal. All similar obstacles are grouped together by using the same number, and rated on a scale of 1 to 5 according to what I would work on first.

2. There's not enough time in our schedules.
1. I'm not interested in what my spouse likes to talk about—the technical details of his work.
2. When we finally find time to talk, we both are too tired to think clearly.
4. My tone of voice seems to turn off my spouse.
3. I feel defensive when we talk.
3. My spouse's ideas seem so important, mine so unimportant.
1. When we talk, I think so hard about what to say next, but nothing comes to mind.
1. Sometimes I seem to have too many things to talk about.
5. I really don't know why my spouse doesn't seem interested in talking with me.

Develop Solutions.   Here comes the easy part. Once you have clearly defined your obstacles or problem areas, the solutions almost write themselves, as shown in the following responses to each obstacle:

1. I will not worry about what I'm going to say. I will simply listen attentively and ask questions. I will try to understand what excites my spouse about his/her work.

2. There *is* time for each other. Certainly I can give fifteen minutes of undivided attention to my spouse. If necessary, I can rest before we talk so I will be at my best. If I share my concern about having time for each other, I'm sure we can come up with creative solutions.

3. The solution to this obstacle is basically a new attitude. I will take the attitude that I don't need to compete with my spouse. I have my own worth as a person. I don't need to prove it. I can feel free to enjoy my spouse and his/her ideas.

4. My negative tone of voice is probably related to my feelings of defensiveness and to my lack of awareness of how I was coming across. I will counteract these tendencies by focusing on my strengths and listening to the tone of my voice as if I were my spouse. I will practice complimenting my spouse daily.

5. If obstacle 5 still exists after taking the above actions, I'll simply share my feelings and ask my spouse what I can do to make our communication mutually satisfying.

Of course, the best solutions to your obstacles are within you. You may, in fact, be surprised to find that your problem-solving ability opens new doors of perception and understanding. In time you may even find the problem-solving process exciting. Then you know you are making progress.

Model Desired Behavior. If you were to select one person who you feel is a model communicator, who would it be? Why is he a model communicator? Specifically, how does he listen? What does his body language convey? What does he signal with his eyes? What kinds of questions does he ask? How does he make his listener feel comfortable? Modeling your behavior after another's strengths is an effective strategy because it is relatively easy to copy a behavior once you see it demonstrated.

Imagine Success. Your mind is a powerful ally. Let it work for you. Write down the benefits you will gain from meeting your goal. Visualize yourself actually expressing your best self. Imagine the delight shown by your conversational partners as they begin to feel understood and want to return the favor.

Write Affirmations. Eliminating negative habits and developing new ones can be frustrating. Most people try, fail, and quit. But if they try, fail, adjust, and try again according to clearly defined goals, they dramatically increase the probabilities of success.

Affirmations give the mental encouragement you may need to "try again." They spur you on in the direction you want to go. They are like cue cards; they keep you on track. Here are some I like:

I am not intimidated by anyone.
I like people and enjoy talking to them.
I am an expert listener.
I share my ideas and feelings with confidence.
When I talk, people listen.
When I fail, I adjust, try again, and succeed.

An important point about affirmations is that they do not need to be presently true in your experience. Rather, they serve as powerful tools to *aid* you in your growth trend. They become true as you repeat them and act on them.

Reward Yourself.   Ignoring our good habits and punishing ourselves for negative habits is a poor way to treat ourselves. It also is counter-productive. Behavioral scientists now are stressing the three R's: Reinforced Responses Recur. This means that if you reward yourself when you implement a new skill and avoid a negative habit, then you actually are strengthening the positive response and increasing your chances of using that skill more often. So think of some way to reward yourself. Anything could be a reward—even something ridiculous like ordering pizza at 3:00 A.M.—whatever will help you savor the feeling of success in achieving your goal.

ACT ON YOUR COMMITMENTS

A survey was made of the New York Lottery "instant millionaires." In almost every case where the recipients had not already made significant achievements in their lives, their money was squandered and soon lost. The missing ingredient? *Commitment*—a dedicated pursuit of a worthwhile personal goal.

Commitment also is essential for eliminating negative habits in communication. Without a strong commitment, defensiveness will screen out valuable insights. Little difficulties in working out communication strategies will become insurmountable obstacles. Here are four commitments that will help you move past obstacles and achieve positive self-expression:

1. I will honestly face my communication problems so I can begin to solve them.
2. I will seek to be all I can be, to accentuate my best self in my communication.
3. I will dare to see myself possessing the power to change and adopt improved ways of relating to people.
4. I will take the action steps necessary to relate to others in the same way I would like them to relate to me.

There is good reason for making these commitments "up front": You learn only what you commit yourself to learn.

When you make these commitments and work on them daily, you will gain victory over the foes of positive change: selfishness, defensiveness, procrastination, and a feeling of worthlessness. As you gain skill in replacing negative habits with purposeful and positive self-expression, your brain will begin to release more of its creative, problem-solving energy. You will catch sight of how you can achieve new levels of understanding and meaning with the significant persons in your life. Your new communication skill will begin to fit you like a tailor-made uniform. It will become a "habit" of successful communication.

ACTION STEPS
FOR WINNING SELF-DIRECTION

1. Make a list of your negative habits in communication. If you can't think of any at first, ask your family or friends. They will be sure to think of some. Don't argue about what they say. Just smile and write. Smile because you know you can eliminate the negative habits. And write them down as your first step toward your goal.

2. Write a SMART goal concerning your communication with a person significant to you. Begin this way: To improve my communication with _____, I will do the following: [List specific steps you feel you need to take].

3. When you experience unsatisfying communication with that person, analyze your words, goals, strategies, and commitments. Under the heading "Negative Habits," write down what you actually said, what your goals were, if any, and so on. Under "Positive Directions," write the changes you will make to improve your communication.

Negative Habits   *Positive Directions*

Words:

Goals:

Strategies:

Commitments:

4. Augment the winning direction you have begun to take by writing simple affirmations on a 3 X 5 card and putting them where you can see them often. For example, "I enjoy talking and listening to _____." "I am becoming the kind of person with whom people enjoy talking." Think and act as if you are getting closer to your communication goals. You are!

4

Learn
the listening art

Listen to me for a day . . . an hour! . . . a moment! lest I expire
in my terrible wilderness, my lonely silence! O God, is there no one
to listen?[1]

SENECA, 4 B.C.

The Bible tells us that Samson killed ten thousand Philistines with the jaw-
bone of an ass. I am convinced that an even greater number of conversations are killed daily with the same instrument.

Ideally, conversations include mutual give and take—a happy medium between talking and listening. Unfortunately, there seem to be a lot
more talkers than listeners. Can you remember the last time you were
trying to make a point and you suddenly noticed that your listener had a
faraway look in his eyes—obviously thinking hard about something? Then
you discovered that rather than paying attention to what you were saying,
he was concentrating on what he would say when you stopped to take a
breath.

Can you name ten people who listen intently to you . . . people who
can think your thoughts after you, empathize with you, and know what
you're trying to say before you put it all into words? Few people can
name five. The great majority of people suffer the loneliness of not being
able to share their true inner selves with persons who will hear them out
and take time to understand.

Why do so few people listen? What is the deep, dark secret about listening that keeps people from mastering this art? There is no secret! There are, however, some simple steps one must take to become a good listener. They are not difficult. Anyone can become an effective listener if he commits himself to practicing each step.

Before we discuss these steps, it is necessary to understand *why* listening well is so important. The Sperry Corporation discovered that without training in the art of listening, we often comprehend only about 25 percent of what we hear. And in both business and personal relationships, the consequences of inadequate listening are extraordinarily costly. Simple listening mistakes cost the business world millions of dollars annually. In personal relationships, simple listening mistakes can lead to communication failures and the tragic breakdown of understanding between people. To illustrate, here is a letter from a runaway teenager.

Dear Folks,

Thank you for everything, but I am going to Chicago and try to start some kind of new life.

You asked me why I did those things and why I gave you so much trouble, and the answer is easy for me to give you, but I am wondering if you will understand.

Remember when I was about six or seven and I used to want you to just listen to me? I remember all the nice things you gave me for Christmas and my birthday and I was really happy with the things . . . for about a week . . . at the time I got the things, but the rest of the time during the year I really didn't want presents, I just wanted all the time for you to listen to me like I was somebody who felt things, too, because I remember even when I was young I felt things. But you said you were busy.

Mom, you are a wonderful cook, and you had everything so clean and you were tired so much from doing all those things that made you busy; but, you know something, Mom? I would have liked crackers and peanut butter just as well if you had only sat down with me a while during the day and said to me: "Tell me all about it so I can maybe help you understand!"

If Donna ever has children, I hope you will tell her to just pay some attention to the one who doesn't smile very much because that one will really be crying inside. And when she's about to bake six dozen cookies, to make sure first that the kids don't want to tell her about a dream or a hope or something, because thoughts are important too to small kids even though they don't have so many words to use when they tell about what they have inside them.

I think that all the kids who are doing so many things that grown-ups are tearing out their hair worrying about are really looking for somebody who will have time to listen a few minutes and who really and truly will treat them as they would a grown-up who might be useful to them; you know, polite to them. If you folks had ever said to me, "Pardon me" when you interrupted me, I'd have dropped dead.

If anybody asks you where I am, tell them I've gone looking for somebody with time because I've got a lot of things I want to talk about.

Love to all,

Your Son[2]

One listening mistake after another—slowly, gradually, imperceptibly—can build a wall of resistance between people.

But listening mistakes need not occur; and positive listening skills can be learned. The Sperry Corporation, which has spent $5 to $6 million annually in listening research and training, reports that in schools where listening has been taught, listening comprehension as much as doubled in just a few months. You will find that you, too, can increase your listening skills when you take the following six steps toward better listening.

STEP ONE: CHOOSE TO LISTEN

Unless we take this first step, we will be stymied by various barriers in our attempts to listen well. Three common barriers to effective listening are particularly bothersome. The first is *stress*. Research indicates that heart problems, cancer, accidents, strokes, lung disease, plus numerous minor ailments have all been attributed, at least in part, to stress. But relationships also are affected. In desperate attempts to recover a bit of peace, the mind seems to race in different directions simultaneously . . . making little or no progress. Such a state makes it very difficult to give full attention to another person unless one makes a definite choice to listen.

A second common listening barrier that needs to be overcome is the *"Me" syndrome.* There seems to be what some social analysts are calling a "new narcissism" abroad in the land, a world view centered on the self, with happiness and personal survival as its sole goal. It is hard to deny that the horizons of millions of Americans have become the limits of their individual concerns. It is this same mood of self-centeredness that has caused some analysts to label the 1970s the "Me" Decade.

When a person is affected by the "Me" syndrome, he doesn't seem to care about the feelings of others. He can't see the legitimacy of any point of view but his own. He listens only to information that will benefit him personally. He hears only what he wants to hear. Deep relationships with others, however much he may want them, do not occur because he is constantly thinking about how to set forth his own ideas, how to justify himself, and how to enhance himself at the expense of others.

A third barrier to good listening is *brain speed.* While an average speech rate for many people is about 200 words per minute, most of us can think about four times that speed. With all that extra think time, the ineffective listener lets his mind wander. His brain takes excursions to review the events of yesterday, or plan tomorrow, or solve a business problem . . . or "sleep."

Each of these three barriers can be overcome by consciously choosing to listen. For example, when the listener makes a firm commitment to listen, he may acknowledge to his partner that he wants to listen, but that he first needs time to relax. His choice to listen gives a clear direction to the mind that will minimize the interference of stress. His choice also will enable him to get beyond self-centered concerns and focus attention on the concerns of the one talking to him. Furthermore, choosing to listen will challenge the brain to capitalize on its extra think time and use its great potential to solve the complexities involved in fully understanding the other person. The good listener *decides* to listen deeply, to glean from both the spoken and silent messages the exact intent and desired response of the one talking to him.

STEP TWO:
LISTEN ACTIVELY

In passive listening the mind is only partially engaged in the communication process. In active listening it is fully engaged. When you listen actively, you concentrate on what is being said and provide empathetic feedback. This encourages the person speaking to continue, to go deeper. Essentially, you are conveying a *language of acceptance*, an unmistakable message that, regardless of your agreement with what is said, the person is important and his thoughts matter.

At a surface level, active listening involves simple responses which open the door for further communication. Here are some "door openers":

Interesting!
Tell me about it.
Tell me more.
Would you like to talk about it?
Let's discuss it.
You have something on your mind.
Your thoughts are important to me.

To go through the open door and achieve deeper understanding you must provide your conversational partner with feedback. Ask for clarification or repeat in your own words what you heard to verify whether your interpretation is the same meaning intended by the sender. Feedback of this kind does not add your evaluations or opinions to the conversation. But it does, with uncanny consistency, encourage your conversational partner to continue, to get to the "heart" of what he feels; and it greatly increases the chance of mutual understanding.

Feedback corrects our normal tendency to make assumptions about what a person means. For example, suppose a child says "I don't want to go back to school." The parent may assume that the child's motive is laziness or that he doesn't want to learn. Moreover, the parent might feel that his authority is being challenged, so he replies with, "Are you crazy? You're going whether you want to or not!" The result? Often it is a battle of wills, perhaps harsh words, loud talk, anger, crying, and unhappiness. But was the conflict necessary?

Consider the following conversation to see how a parent arrived at a truer understanding of the child's need and avoided unnecessary conflict through active listening:

Child: I don't want to go to school!
Parent: You don't want to go to school.
Child: I hate school.
Parent: You don't like to do schoolwork?
Child: No, it's not the work. It's the other kids.
Parent: The other kids.
Child: Yes . . . especially Rick, Tom, and Steve.
Parent: You don't like Rick, Tom, and Steve?
Child: They don't like me!
Parent: I see.
Child: They make fun of me and call me "Crazy Legs."
Parent. "Crazy Legs?"
Child: They think I run funny.
Parent: Did you know there was a famous football player people called "Crazy Legs" Hirsch?
Child: No . . . really?
Parent: Yes. He seemed to run differently than most players. Yet he was hard to stop.
Child: I can run pretty fast.
Parent: Yes. I know you can. . . . It's time for school now. Better get going.
Child: OK.

Although this conversation is condensed, consider its effectiveness. What did the parent do? What change occurred in the child's image of himself? Active listening has the power to dissolve defensiveness, heal hurt feelings, and improve self-esteem. At first this approach may seem unrealistic and awkward. But it really works. Try it consistently for even one week. What could you lose? Better yet, what could you gain?

Cases of misunderstanding are usually so difficult because we are not aware that we are misunderstanding the true intentions of another person. We assume our judgments are correct. The problem is further complicated by the fact that an individual may misjudge not only the other, but also *his own feelings.* The child thought at first that his feeling of discomfort was directed at school, then at three classmates. The real reason for his uneasiness was his concept of himself in relation to the three classmates. When he changed (improved) his image of himself, his attitude toward school changed. It would have been difficult for the child to have discovered his true feeling and improved his self-concept without the active help of his parent.

To listen actively, keep in mind the following:

1. Begin active listening when you notice statements that convey deep emotion, don't make sense, seem to have no connection to the matter at hand, or are ironic, cynical, self-depreciating, critical.
2. Listen actively when there seems to be more than one meaning to a statement or you are not sure your interpretation of a statement is accurate.
3. Avoid manipulation or using active listening as a new way of nagging.
4. Do not simply parrot words or facts, but try to reflect the meaning or feeling of a statement.
5. Develop a sense of timing. Attempting to listen actively may be futile when one's spouse has just come home exhausted from work and does not want to talk.

Active listening is the best way to get at what someone really feels and thus avoid useless argument or miscommunication.

STEP THREE:
LISTEN FOR IDEAS AND FEELINGS

According to Archie Bunker, Edith has a problem listening to him on his level. "The reason you don't understand me, Edith, is because I'm talking to you in English and you're listening in dingbat!"[3] We listen in "dingbat" whenever we hear only clichés and facts and fail to understand the ideas or feelings conveyed.

Not all listening is of the same kind or at the same level. It doesn't need to be. We don't listen to a TV commercial with the same intensity as we do a person who says "I love you." Being aware of the various levels of listening can help us to determine the level we are on and evaluate whether it is adequate.

Five levels of listening can be diagramed this way:

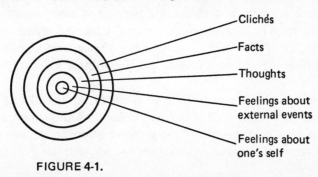

FIGURE 4-1.

Clichés are phrases without much meaning, such as "Hi . . . How are you? . . . Fine . . . You? . . . Nice day . . . Yes, lovely weather . . . So what's new?" Perhaps you have heard about people taking advantage of cliché listening for fun. When asked, "How are you?" they might respond, "I feel like I'm going to die." The listener responds automatically with "Great! Have a nice day." Normally clichés serve as agents of minimum politeness, but they can also function as door openers, leading the conversation to a deeper level. When you ask "How are you?" you can show genuine interest in knowing the full answer.

Facts generally deal with external events. "Scientists are still debating whether the Viking lander detected signs of life on Mars." "Judson made an A in spelling." A great deal of conversation and listening takes place at this level.

Thoughts represent one's interpretation of events or facts. "I think our taxation system is unfair to middle income people." "I believe the economy shows signs of a healthy recovery." "We can't really lose money if we buy this house now." One's thoughts tell us something about how another person sorts out reality. Often we listen to thoughts to determine whether we agree or disagree with the other person's views.

Feelings can be divided roughly into two categories: feelings about external events and feelings about one's self. Both types of feelings can become very intense. For example, one might assert with a tone of outrage: "I feel that abortion is murder!" "I feel that women are still being discriminated against!" Feelings about one's self can go one step deeper, often reflecting fear, guilt, or hurt: "I now feel that the abortion I had was murder." I feel that I am being discriminated against at work." Because of their intensity, listening to feelings is sometimes threatening and hard work. We are put on the spot. We sense that if we respond the wrong way to one's feelings, either we will be verbally attacked or we will further hurt someone already in a vulnerable position. Consequently, afraid of being caught in a no-win situation, we pull back and refuse to hear the deepest feelings of another. The problem is that it works both ways. To the extent that we refuse to listen deeply, others are likely to refuse to listen to us.

The good listener is not afraid to listen for ideas and feelings. (The real threat occurs when we fail to listen deeply.) Although negative ideas and feelings may tend to provoke a negative response in you—especially when they are directed *against* you—you can set your mind on the following principles and determine to enhance the possibility of listening enrichment:

1. As a listener, you can refuse to evaluate or judge the speaker. You can simply, genuinely listen.
2. When you feel you are being judged, you might tell your partner, "I do not want to judge you, nor do I expect to be judged. If our conversation can proceed on that basis, I will listen intently."
3. Aim for understanding and cooperation, not manipulation and control. Openly clarify your motives if your partner seems to be unaware of them.
4. Don't be afraid of deep feelings. Don't react to them as if they represented unchanging truth. Feelings change, sometimes in a moment. What is said in a fit of anger or frustration may be completely contrary to the abiding values and commitments of an individual. In most cases, however, the release of deep feelings is therapeutic and enables the sender to return to a truer representation of himself.
5. When feelings become too strong for you to listen effectively, tell your partner that you need a break and set a mutually acceptable time when dialogue can resume.

STEP FOUR: LISTEN WITH THE HEART'S "EAR"

Hearing is not the same as *listening* even though we often use the words interchangeably. *Hearing* refers to a *physiological* process by which auditory impressions are received by the ears and transmitted to the brain.

Consider for a moment what a fascinating process hearing is. The outer ear, sculptured like a sound trumpet, catches sound waves and guides them into the auditory canal. At the end of the canal, the waves vibrate the eardrum, sending vibrations across the three bones of the middle ear and moving the innermost bone in and out. Then a fluid translates sound waves into nerve impulses and stimulates nerves to send messages to the hearing center in the brain. Remarkable! Even scientists do not know exactly how this hearing mechanism tells the difference between sounds of different pitch!

Greater still is the process of listening. *Listening* refers to an even more complex *psychological* procedure involving interpreting and understanding the significance of the sensory experience. A baby's cry, the

roar of the ocean, an inspiring speech, the music of a great symphony—
these and other sounds produce within us feelings, thoughts, and actions
that can immeasurably enrich our lives.

Listen literally means to list, to lean to one side. A person intent on
understanding another may actually *lean* toward him and be *inclined*
mentally and emotionally to interpret correctly the sender's point of
view. The opposite of listening is to be listless, indifferent, not inclined
to understand. In our conversation we are listening or listless, or somewhere in between.

To move beyond simply hearing sounds to listening with the "ear"
of the heart, two personality characteristics need to be cultivated. First,
empathy—the projection of one's own personality into the personality of
the other in order to understand him better. For example, the listener
might ask himself, "How would I feel if I were in the other person's situation? If I had to live in his house, work with his boss, earn his salary, care
for his kids, respond to his wife, deal with his problems . . . would I have
the same feelings he is expressing to me now?" Empathy is walking
through experiences in the other person's shoes; it is trying to see the
world through his eyes—*not* for the purpose of agreement or changing
your own perspective on an issue, although that might happen—but for the
purpose of understanding the other as fully as possible.

A second quality necessary for listening with the heart's ear is
acceptance of your conversational partner as he or she is. In some cases
this is most difficult to do because we don't like what the partner has done
or said. We want to change him, remake him into our own image of acceptability. Yet acceptance of the person is usually a prerequisite to his
change. Acceptance of the other person is easier if we make a mental
distinction between the person and his actions. There is very great difference between thinking that a person's *actions* have resulted in failure and
thinking that the *person* is a failure. If we can maintain an attitude of
acceptance toward the person even when we dislike his actions, we will be
psychologically much more ready to listen.

STEP FIVE: LISTEN TO YOURSELF

William Shakespeare wrote: "Go to your bosom, knock there and ask your
heart what it doth know."[4] We give ear to our children and spouse, to a
speech, to television and radio programs, to friends and to a thousand
other voices—but neglect to listen to the voice within. If one does not take

the time to know his own mind, to explore his own innermost feelings, to hear himself out regarding certain issues, to understand his own dreams and ambitions, he is not likely to do so with anyone else.

The capacity to listen to one's self provides the sense of personal integration and psychological readiness necessary to be open or receptive to another point of view. Wendell Johnson reflects on this point in *Your Most Enchanted Listener*:

> A man is never so serene as when he hears himself out, granting to himself the quieting freedom to speak fully without fear of self reproach. Nor is he so gravely ill as when he stops his tongue with crying out "Shame! Shame!" unto himself.... By stopping up our ears against the sound of our own voices we achieve not the peace of inner stillness, but the unnerving disquietude of haunted consciousness.[5]

When you listen carefully to yourself you realize how you come across to other people. Have you ever taken a recording of an informal conversation, played it back, and then had someone remark, "I didn't know I sounded like that. Is there something wrong with the recorder?" I am convinced that innumerable parents have never listened to the tone of their voice when talking to their own children. They do not hear the verbal abuse. They cannot imagine why their "harmless" remark makes another upset.

Listening to one's self can be threatening precisely because it can reveal areas of the personality that need change. It is possible to listen to one's heart and be shocked by the ugliness imprisoned there. But discovery *can* lead to constructive change. If one chooses to change, to acknowledge faults and inadequacies, and to begin to eradicate them through positive commitments and actions—then he is on his way to becoming a whole person. The pop psychology that only tells people what they want to hear, that tells them how good they are ... merely puts Band-Aids on the soul. Surgery may be necessary before healing can occur.

As you listen to yourself, what do you hear that you want to change? What do you want to develop further?

STEP SIX: KNOW WHEN TO KEEP SILENT

Silence communicates, but the messages vary. The silence of *retreat* is the sulking attitude which says, "I don't need to talk to you. I'll just think my own thoughts and isolate myself from you." The silence of *anger* is the attempt to get even, to lash out by keeping thoughts within, to refuse to give one the pleasure of company. Then there is the silence of *awkwardness* which almost shouts, "Help! Let me out of here! I don't know what to say! Somebody say something!" There is also the silence of *support.* Instead of filling up time with small talk, that silence says: "I want to take the time to hear you without interrupting you. I want to know how you feel about yourself, your failures, your accomplishments, your future plans." What a great experience to be on the other end of that kind of silence!

Your supportive silence can help a friend in crisis. Although persons with serious psychological problems should be referred to trained, competent therapists, almost anyone can help a friend in crisis if he cultivates effective listening skills. The most common (and serious) error of the helper is trying to *solve* the problem for the friend. The misguided helper readily gives advice, instructions, logic, and guidance in hopes of relieving the friend's burden. When this doesn't work, the "helper" sometimes resorts to ridicule, sarcasm, joking, and playing down the seriousness of the problem. But it is supportive silence that has the power to help and heal.

In my counseling I am amazed at the therapeutic power of silent, supportive listening. One counselee echoed hundreds when she said: "Thanks for your help! I feel so much better now." What did I do? What gems of wisdom did I offer to change a depressed and anxious person into a calm and confident person once again? I said very little. I simply listened skillfully.

In the course of several years the Baylys lost three of their children. In his book *The Last Thing We Talk About*, Joe Bayly shares his feelings about two kinds of friends who tried to help when one of the children died:

> I was sitting, torn by grief. Someone came and talked to me of God's dealings, of why it happened, of hope beyond the grave. He talked constantly. He said things I knew were true.
>
> I was unmoved, except to wish he'd go away. He finally did.
>
> Another came and sat beside me. He didn't talk. He didn't ask me leading questions. He just sat beside me for an hour and more, listened when I said something, answered briefly, prayed simply, left.
>
> I was moved. I was comforted. I hated to see him go.[6]

ACTION STEPS
FOR WINNING SELF-DIRECTION

1. List the names of people who deeply listen to you.

2. List reasons why some people don't listen to you very well (e.g., "I talk more than a minute at a time." "I don't show much interest in the other person's views"). What can you do about it?

3. In reference to the five levels of listening mentioned in this chapter, at what level do you tend to listen? Is that level adequate for the kind of relationships you want to build and experience?

4. Listen to yourself by asking yourself what your dreams, ambitions, and innermost thoughts are. Record your answers in a "Thought Journal."

5. Plan time to listen deeply to a family member or friend. Write down the mutual benefits both of you would experience.

6. On a scale of 1 (poor) to 100 (excellent), how would you rate yourself as a listener? _____

7. How would the following people rate you?

Mother _____   Employer _____

Father _____   Employee _____

Spouse _____   Friends _____

Children _____

8. List three or more steps you intend to take to increase your listening ability. Act on them today.

5

Discover how communication works

I know you believe you understand what you think I said, but I am not sure you realize that what you heard is not what I meant!

ANONYMOUS

Communication breakdowns are difficult to repair because there are so many reasons why they occur. When we don't know precisely what the problem is and have no method to aid the mind in discovering relevant information, it is as if we are lost in unfamiliar territory without a map.

A model of the communication process is like a map. A map simplifies a large geographical area in a way that allows us to study it and find the way we want to go. Likewise, a model of the communication process simplifies a very complex process to the point where we can examine it, discover how to avoid paths that lead to dead-end dialogues, and pursue the ways that lead toward understanding. Models, like maps, do not tell us what to do, but they help us see the best way to get back on track and reach our goal.

Just as a city map will not help us travel across the country, so also in communication one model is not enough to give us an adequate picture of what happens in our conversations. In this chapter, we will use three diagnostic models designed to help us solve communication problems and prevent others from occurring. We will analyze:

1. The major components in the communication process:
2. The interactive nature of our communications using the method of transactional analysis, and
3. How the broader context of life situations affects our communications.

Each model will contain simple questions to aid us in locating a problem and increasing understanding.

COMPONENT ANALYSIS

The first model focuses on the major components of the communication process: (1) the person who speaks, (2) the speech that he produces, and (3) the person who listens. Although each of these parts affects the others, we will view them in their simplest relationships as follows:

FIGURE 5-1.

A breakdown in communication could occur in any one of these components or in a combination of them.

As we look at each component separately, focus your attention on your role relative to each component. For example, ask yourself these questions:

1. How do I, as the *speaker*, contribute to a communication problem?
2. How does what I say and the way I say it affect the transfer of my *message*?
3. How do I, as the *listener*, contribute to a communication problem?

1. Speaker Problems. Probably nothing affects the quality of a communication more than the personality of the speaker, that is, who he is individually and who he is in relationship to the listener. For example, if

the speaker is honest, sincere, and well liked, his message will tend to be well received. If he is perceived as untrustworthy, his message will likely be rejected, regardless of its clarity, logic, or eloquence.

In Chapter 2 we looked at seven personality characteristics that contribute to failure in communication. Here we will limit our attention to one major problem that combines several of those characteristics: shyness. Philip Zimbardo, author of *Shyness* and director of the Stanford Shyness Clinic, estimates that there are 84,000,000 people in the United States who consider themselves shy—that's 40 percent of the population! Shyness is a shrinking from human contact often because of a feeling of inferiority and fear of taking risks. Shyness is an alienating force that prevents people from realizing their full potential with other people and results in excessive preoccupation with their own feelings. Shy people tend to sell themselves short, to have low self-esteem, and to cause other people to evaluate them negatively. Ironically, negative evaluations are exactly what they want to avoid. But because they fear rejection, they tend to stay away from other people, and this very act often causes rejection.

If shyness is a problem at times for you, or if you wrestle with other personality problems, the following strategies can help increase your effectiveness as a communicator.

• Accept yourself as a person with something worthwhile to say. Stand tall, look directly in the other person's eyes, convey the message that you are not afraid.

• Listen to yourself talk as if you were another person. Ask yourself if you sound ego-centered, shy, or defensive.

• Avoid judging another person. Instead, ask for more information when you come to a point of contention. Remember that people are complex—we don't see the motives for their behavior. Cultivate tolerance.

• Pay attention to your behavior and how it affects your listener. Habits such as scratching your head, not looking at your listener, staring, mocking, and so on can be enormously irritating.

• Choose to control your emotions. Begin to think of yourself as one who can change even long-standing patterns. Fill your mind with reasons why a change would be worthwhile. Resist feeling sorry for yourself or concentrating on past failures. Visualize yourself in control of your emotions and the benefits you would gain from such control. Program yourself mentally and emotionally for constructive responses to aggravating situations.

• Begin changing what you can change. Decide which patterns you have that are nonproductive and begin to eliminate them. Dare to let another person know that you are in the process of changing.

• Expect positive change to occur, even if it is gradual. Visualize yourself communicating successfully. Work toward that goal.

2. Message Problems.   One common problem with our messages is word selection. A few years ago, the misuse of a single word in Middle East negotiations almost stirred up another war. Domestic fights can also be started by poor word choice. Mark Twain was correct when he remarked, "The difference between the right word and the almost right word is the difference between lightning and the lightning bug."[1]

Beyond problems in selecting the right words, we encounter difficulties in the relationship of one sentence or thought to the next. The progression of thought may be as clear as ABC in our minds, so clear in fact that our minds might skip B for the sake of efficiency. But the same progression of thought might not be clear to the listener. When the B part of the progression is skipped over, the potential for misunderstanding increases. Unclear communication often reflects unclear thinking. If we speak without thinking, we cannot speak with exactness.

Messages that include "garbage dumping" (putdowns, complaints, sarcasm, ridicule, name-calling) turn communication off. That fact should be obvious, but common experience shows that many people deliberately dump such trash on family, neighbors, and business associates, and then seem surprised when their messages backfire. Perhaps they do not really consider how the epithet "Stupid!" makes a child or spouse feel. They do not catch the irony of screaming "Shut up!" at the kids. They seem to forget that when they judge, they get judged.

Sometimes people resort to garbage dumping, a negative means, to achieve a positive end. A father might tell his son he is "dumb" or "lazy"— not because his goal is to hurt feelings, but because he really wants to motivate his boy to succeed. A wife might complain about how badly she feels—not because she wants to be a burden, but because she wants attention. A daughter may yell that she "hates" her mother—not because she really does, but because she is frustrated and dissatisfied with herself. Often people are not aware of the damaging power of such messages.

Even when our thoughts and words are clear and constructive, we sometimes have difficulty controlling the message medium, or *how* we convey the message. Research suggests that in face-to-face conversations, 7 percent of a message depends on words, 23 percent on the tone of voice, and 70 percent on nonverbal body language! In *A Couple's Guide to Communication*,[2] John Gottman provides a list of the positive and negative features of facial expressions, voice cues, and body positions and movements that can help us determine how we convey our messages:

FACIAL EXPRESSIONS

Positive Face	Negative Face	
smile	frown	mocking laughter
laughter	sneer	smirk
empathic face	cry	angry face
head nod	glare	disgust
eye contact		

VOICE CUES

Positive Voice		Negative Voice	
caring	satisfied	cold	blaming
warm	buoyant	tense	sarcastic
soft	bubbly	scared	angry
tender	cheerful	impatient	furious
relieved	chuckling	hard	blaring
empathic	happy	clipped	hurt
concerned	joyful	staccato	depressed
affectionate	laughing	whining	accusing
loving			

BODY POSITIONS AND MOVEMENTS

Positive Body	Negative Body
touching	neck or hand tension
distance reduction	rude gestures
open arms	throw up hands in disgust
attention	point
relaxation	jab
forward lean	inattention

Look at each of the key words a second time and put a checkmark next to those positive characteristics that you want to develop more fully.

The following strategies are designed to help you gain greater control over what you say and how you say it:

• Check to see if the listener understands. Encourage questions. Never stifle the listener with "Stupid!" or the like. Ask, "Am I making myself clear?" "Do you know what I mean?"

• Think before you speak. Avoid hasty generalizations. Ask yourself if there is a clear, reasonable connection between your statements.

• Say precisely what you mean. Don't expect your listener to understand a hidden message. If the hidden message is worth saying, dare to say it clearly.

• Try not to repeat. Condense your message and avoid speaking for more than a minute at a time.

• Ask yourself, "How am I making the other person feel? Would *I* like to feel that way? How could I have said that better?" Become aware that putdown messages are usually damaging not only to communication, but to the other's self-esteem as well.

• Listen to the tone quality and volume of your voice. Is it harsh, too loud, irritating? Modulate your voice so it sounds pleasing to you. Do not speak louder than necessary.

• Consider your body and facial expressions. Check them in a mirror if possible. Ask yourself, "How is what I'm saying coming through?" Am I tense? Do I look worried, uncertain, angry?"

3. Listener Problems. Inattention by the listener may be produced by any number of factors, including his fatigue, preoccupation with something or someone else, or disagreement with the message. Three of the most troublesome listener problems are judgmental reactions, maintaining a different frame of reference, and unresolved conflicts with the speaker.

Judgmental reactions by a listener seriously block the flow of conversation. In a speech on communication, psychologist Carl Rogers stated that "the major barrier to mutual interpersonal communication is our very natural tendency to judge, to evaluate, to approve or disapprove the statement of the other person, or the other group."[3] Here is the point Carl

Rogers makes: we evaluate on the basis of *our* point of view, *our* point of reference. We assume that our grasp of a particular situation is the only true and correct one. The result is that we fail to listen with understanding. Rogers maintains that real communication means

> to see the expressed idea and attitude from the other person's point of view, to sense how it feels to him, to achieve his frame of reference in regard to the thing he is talking about. Understanding *with* a person—not *about* him—is such an effective approach that it can bring about major changes in personality.[4]

Communication also breaks down when a listener has a *different frame of reference* than the speaker. A frame of reference is a selected set of standards by which words, ideas, or behavior are considered meaningful and appropriate or inappropriate. The "generation gap," for example, is caused in part by different frames of reference. An exaggerated and comic example of the problem is illustrated in Mark Twain's short story, "Buck Fanshaw's Funeral." Scotty is merely trying to arrange a funeral for a friend, but both Scotty and the minister show a lack of awareness of each other's frame of reference.

> "Are you the duck that runs the gospel mill next door?"
> "Am I the—pardon me, I believe I do not understand."
> With another sigh and a half sob, Scotty rejoined:
> "Why, you see we are in a bit of trouble, and the boys thought maybe you would give us a lift, if we'd tackle you—that is, if I've got the rights of it and you are the head clerk of the doxology works next door."
> "I am the shepherd in charge of the flock whose fold is next door."
> "The which?"
> "The spiritual adviser of the little company of believers whose sanctuary adjoins these premises."
> Scotty scratched his head, reflected a moment, and then said:
> "You ruther hold over me, pard. I reckon I can't call that hand. Ante and pass the buck."
> "How? I beg pardon. What did I understand you to say?"
> "Well, you've ruther got the bulge on me. Or maybe we've both got the bulge, somehow. You don't smoke me and I don't smoke you. You see, one of the boys has passed in his checks and we want to give him a good send-off, and so the thing I'm on now is to roust out

somebody to jerk a little chin music for us and waltz him through handsome."

"My friend, I seem to grow more and more bewildered. Your observations are wholly incomprehensible to me. Cannot you simplify them in some way? At first I thought perhaps I understood you, but I grope now. Would it not expedite matters if you restricted yourself to categorical statements of fact unencumbered with obstructing accumulations of metaphor and allegory?"[5]

Different frames of reference need not cause misunderstanding. When you are open to the other person's frame of reference, the differences between you can open up new vistas of knowledge and appreciation of each person's uniqueness. None of us sees the world from the same point of view. That makes communication necessary . . . and interesting.

A third listener problem occurs when the listener has an *unresolved conflict* with the speaker. The conflict may cause such a great psychological distance that neither party is able to "hear" the other. Leon Festinger's experiments on cognitive dissonance show that even though a message positively reflects a speaker's thought, it will likely be negatively received if the relationship between speaker and listener is negative. We can diagram it this way:

FIGURE 5-2.

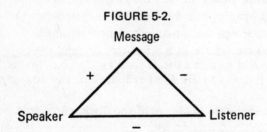

In other words, if a schoolteacher dislikes an administrator, he will find plenty wrong with the administrator's messages. If there is an unresolved conflict between a husband and wife, everything one spouse says will tend to be negatively interpreted by the other.

As a listener, you can significantly increase your communication effectiveness by following these strategies.

• If for some reason you find yourself unable to listen well, say to the one speaking, "I'm not able to listen right now. Let's talk later."

• Imagine the speaker's message to be like a page in a book. Unless you turn it, you see only one side. Acknowledge to yourself that you don't know the message adequately unless you see it from the speaker's viewpoint as well as you own.

• Ask for clarification until you get it.

• Work at conflict resolution with the speaker. If the conflict cannot be readily resolved, deal with it later. Time might be necessary for healing. Talk about the conflict openly as soon as you can. Seek professional help if the conflict persists.

Component analysis is like looking at snapshots of the major parts of the communication process. It allows us to study details of a problem area. But there is also a dynamic flow and variation to our communications. To understand those variations, we can use the model of transactional analysis.

TRANSACTIONAL ANALYSIS

Transactional analysis (TA) provides an effective tool to understand the *interactive nature* of communication. As popularized by Thomas Harris in *I'm OK–You're OK*, TA helps us to discover how and why personality variations sometimes frustrate our attempts at communication and what to do about it.

In TA theory, persons are said to normally exhibit three types of personality expression, *regardless of their age*, which are designated as Parent, Adult, and Child (P, A, C). These designations describe certain recognizable types of expression or "ego states." If we were to use a TA model to diagram most of our conversation patterns, they would look like this:

FIGURE 5-3.

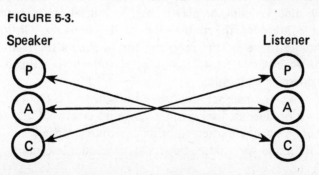

Speaker   Listener

Note that the way the sender expresses his personality (as P, A, or C) suggests the way in which the receiver is likely to respond. For example, if the sender speaks as a Parent, the receiver is influenced by that conversation to respond as a Child.

In TA theory, Adult expression is honest and nondefensive, treats the listener with consideration and respect, and draws out the listener's best and most mature qualities. An Adult-to-Adult pattern emerges when:

> A mother talks with her child as she would to a good friend, conveying acceptance and trust.
>
> A husband shares with his wife a decision he must make in business and invites her perspective on the matter.
>
> A teenage son sits down for a "man-to-man" talk with his father.

In such communication there might be serious differences, but they are not an obstacle to understanding. The characteristics of Adult-to-Adult communication are mutuality, respect, openness. When this kind of expression occurs, it is extremely satisfying.

More often it seems that communication follows the lines of Parent-Child or Child-Parent. (Remember that in TA theory, these designations do not refer to age level, but to the quality or character of the "transactions" between persons.) A Parent-Child transaction in communication often includes a demanding, scolding tone of voice, an authoritarian attitude that attempts to raise the status of the speaker and belittle the status of the listener. A father comes home and demands that his wife clean up the house, or calls his son "Birdbrain" because he forgot to mow the lawn, or yells at his daughter because she forgot to do something he asked her to do. A wife nags her husband about jobs to be done around the house or screams commands to the children. A six-year-old mimics the same screams and commands in his attempt to control a younger (or sometimes older) sibling or playmate. The crucial factor here is not so much the content of the transaction as its *character*. Obviously, it is uncomfortable to be on the receiving end of such a transaction. No one likes to be yelled at or belittled, and the person who is acting like a Parent probably doesn't like it either.

All of us at times act childish. Although in TA theory the Child is sometimes spontaneous, lively, fun-loving, and creative, Child reactions to not getting one's way are often emotional outbursts, anger, and frustration. In the Child mode we want to be served, coddled, the center of attention, free of responsibility. Sometimes we even want to be told what to do or how to think. We put ourselves in dependent and often self-defeating situations. A college student puts off until the last minute study for an exam or work on a term paper and then complains he did not get a fair grade. A girl becomes indignant when her date is late and doesn't let him forget it. A motorist works himself into a rage because an older couple is driving too slowly in front of him, and he vents his anger for the next half-hour by driving too fast. A wife or husband is too easily offended and withdraws into a shell of silent rebuke.

Anger, resentment, hurt feelings, defensiveness, a low tolerance level for frustration—these can block communication. Yet these feelings are also important to express on an Adult-to-Adult level. Resolution and healing are most likely to occur as a result of such sharing and understanding.

Here is the point of this kind of analysis: It can help us diagnose more accurately the areas in which we contribute to communication failure. For example, my behavior—which has been strongly affected by the behavior of the other person—is in turn influencing the way *he* sees himself and consequently how he will respond to me next. If I am not aware of the nature of these transactions, I can become bitterly entangled in a network of unpleasant communication patterns and not have the foggiest notion how to get out. But if I can assess my part in the negative transactions, I will understand how to improve the quality of my communication.

Use the following questions to aid your mind in assessing your own transactions:

1. Under what conditions do I tend to communicate as Adult, Parent, or Child? For example, consider the time of day, with whom you are talking, and the place in which you talk.
2. How does my manner of communication affect the way the listener responds to me?
3. How does the other person's manner of communication influence the way I respond to him or her?

As you gather information through your transactional analysis, put it to work in ways that will improve the quality of your interactions with other people. The following strategies show the steps to take toward that goal:

- In conversations that seem to be ineffective, ask yourself: "Am I acting like a Parent, Child, or Adult? How do I want to come across?"

• Recognize that there may be connections between your present ego state and all of the past emotional experiences still lingering in your memory. A feeling of "I'm not OK" might be caused not by the present, but by the past. Decide to act in the present against inhibiting or crippling feelings of the past.

• Analyze how you respond to remarks from someone else. For example, if someone pays you a compliment, how do you react? Do you get wordy? Ignore it? Stammer? Change the topic? Ask yourself, "Why do I respond that way? Do I really want to move out of the tyranny of the past and exercise self-direction in the present?"

• Put the Adult in you in charge. Avoid using dogmatic Parent words like *should, shouldn't, always, never, nonsense* or Child vocabulary punctuated by "I want," "I need," "I wish," "I won't," "I can't," "Give me." Use Adult expressions that convey openness, flexibility, positive assertiveness, sensitivity to the other's point of view.

• Bring out the best qualities in the person with whom you are talking. Concentrate on enabling a listener to change from a Child or Parent to an Adult by maintaining your own Adult ego state and treating him with respect even when he seems to be asking for punishment or tries to manipulate or dominate the conversation. Keep in mind that because communication is a transaction, what you give will be very similar to what you get.

Suppose a husband and wife become involved in a verbal fight during supper. If we were to analyze the "transactions" between them, we might learn a great deal about why the argument occurred, but not the whole story. For a fuller understanding, we would need to know some of the experiences of each person before the argument. The same is true in our communication. To understand how our context or situation influences our conversations, we turn to Life-Space Analysis.

LIFE-SPACE ANALYSIS

Each of us lives within a particular life-space or context. My life-space is not the same as yours and yours is not the same as anyone else's. Our context is the world as we know it. We are a part of that world and it is a part of us.

We do not really understand another person well—where he's "coming from" and what he means—unless we know something about his life space. Psychologist Kurt Lewin and others have contended that a person cannot be adequately understood unless he is known in relationship to his environment. Employers want to know not only an applicant's personality, but also his educational and vocational background. A presidential candidate is examined not only on his grasp of the issues and how he would handle them, but on his voting record and just about everything else in his past that seems relevant. Our context gives people clues as to who we are and what we mean when we talk.

A simple model for analyzing a person's life-space is to view that person as an identity surrounded and influenced by six major areas of his life:

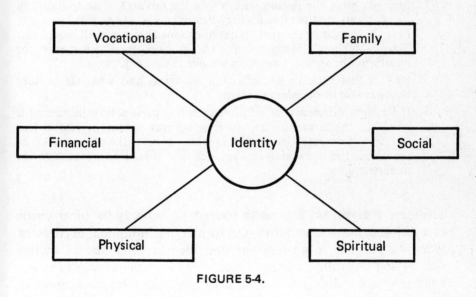

FIGURE 5-4.

These areas or categories are few enough to remember and major enough to lead us into greater detail if necessary. Each is part of an interlocking system. A problem in one area is likely to affect other areas. For example, a communication problem at work may be due to financial pressure, fatigue, anxiety about a teenage daughter, shyness, or an over-whelming fear of death.

With limited knowledge of an individual's life situation, the chances of misjudging him and misunderstanding his message are significantly increased. If a manager assumes that an employee's anger is directed to-ward him personally, he may become defensive or even fire the employee. Life-space analysis might reveal that the anger was caused by five over-draft notices the employee had received from the bank or that a fellow employee's poor work reflected negatively on his own performance.

When we ask ourselves the following life-space questions about another person, we can learn significant information that will help us to solve communication problems:

1. What particular context or life-space dimension is most relevant to understanding the person with whom I'm talking? What do I already know about that area of his life? For example, has he just lost a job, been promoted or married? What questions about himself would this person welcome? (Many persons are far more open to and eager for questions about their lives than we give them credit for.)

2. How is this person's life situation changing, and what affect does that have on our communication?

3. If I have a difference of opinion with this person, how important is it within the larger context of time and my system of values? Has our discussion revealed the total picture of what the other thinks, or are there thoughts and feelings not yet shared but necessary for understanding.

Life-space analysis can help us to understand not only the other person in a dialogue, but also ourselves—our own anger, frustration, or concerns. When we are able to analyze our own life-space and that of another quickly and efficiently, we gain a broader, more accurate image of what is happening in our dialogues and the ability to make them more enjoyable. We are likely to improve our discernment of the topic under discussion and know what next to say about it. Remember the fable of the six blind men who tried to understand what an elephant was like? One felt the elephant's leg and declared that the elephant was a tree. Another felt his tail and insisted it was rope, etc. If the blind men had used a systematic method for altering their perspectives and moving from one part of the elephant to another, they could have increased their understanding of the elephant . . . and each other.

SUMMARY

In this chapter we have focused on three ways to analyze and solve communication problems—through component, transactional, and life-space analysis. Component analysis uses a "snapshot" approach to study the speaker, the message, and the listener. Transactional analysis takes a "motion picture" review of the way communication partners respond to each other (as an Adult, Parent, or Child). Life-space analysis takes a "panoramic" view of the environment or total situation which affects the way a person communicates. Each model by itself yields helpful, but partial information. But when the models are used together as complementary perspectives, they provide a fuller understanding of a communication problem and how to solve it. They help us break down imposing communication barriers and then provide the foundation for a new synthesis of communication-building strategies.

Basic to each of the three models is a set of questions designed to aid the mind in gathering relevant information for problem solving. A recap of these questions shows the particular focus on each model.

Component Analysis

1. How do I as the *speaker* contribute to a communication problem?
2. How does what I say and the way I say it affect the transfer of my *message*?
3. How do I as the *listener* contribute to a communication problem?

Transactional Analysis

1. Under what conditions can my communications be described as Adult, Parent, or Child?
2. How does my manner of communication affect the way the listener responds to me?
3. How does the other person's manner of communication influence the way I respond to him or her?

Life-Space Analysis

1. What particular context or life-space dimension is most relevant to understanding the person with whom I'm talking?

2. How is this person's life situation changing and what effect does that have on our communication?

3. If we have a difference of opinion, how important is it within the larger context of time and my system of values?

Persistent use of these models will generate increased options and result in better choices in what to say and how to say it. In other words, we will be able to guard against too narrow a view and will be able to see not only the trees, but also the forest—and its changing shades of color as well. Aided by such an approach, conversation will consistently avoid the impasse, the unwanted wrangling, the psychological distance. Instead, it will increase the number and quality of features we want to share, the deeper thoughts and the mountaintop feelings.

ACTION STEPS
FOR WINNING SELF-DIRECTION

1. Turn to the questions related to component analysis in the summary of this chapter and ask yourself the three questions. Focus your attention on a specific and recent communication problem as you reflect on these questions. Don't labor over the analysis. Write down the first thoughts that come to your mind (e.g. "I realize now that my messages have not been clear and direct"). Your analysis is like a road map: It shows you where you got lost and how to get back on track to reach your destination.

2. Use the questions in the summary related to transactional analysis as a means of discovering how you change from one conversational pattern to another (i.e., Adult, Parent, Child). Ask yourself these questions when communication breaks down to check how you're coming through and to determine whether or not you need to change your conversational pattern.

3. When you feel comfortable with component and transactional analysis, ask yourself the questions related to lifespace analysis. Instead of a city or state map, this analysis is like a map of the entire country. Use it to get a broader, more complete picture of the person(s) you want to understand. Use it especially when you find it difficult to accept the person with whom you're talking.

Win
people's attention

To be human at all is to speak, however poorly, and to be human at best is to speak exceptionally well.[1]

WENDELL JOHNSON

If you enter conversations with the attitude that "I'm going to talk in such a way that the other person will be glad he listened," you will win attention. Your positive frame of mind will motivate you to talk and listen in ways that attract people. You will not find yourself saying:

> "My husband never listens to me."
> "I talk to my son until I'm blue in the face, but it doesn't do any good."
> "If I've told you once, I've told you a thousand times. . ."
> "No one ever asks me what I think."

However, you may find that even when you speak exceptionally well, you lose the attention of others occasionally. People are too full of their own concerns to always give undivided attention. But lack of interest in what you say can be kept to a minimum and conversation can be mutually satisfying when you act on the following principles developed in this chapter.

1. Avoid conversation killers.
2. Develop your thoughts on interesting topics.
3. Learn how to ask questions.
4. Memorize surefire conversation starters.
5. Remember names.
6. Practice the skills of good conversation.

AVOID CONVERSATION KILLERS

Perfectly happy conversation can suddenly be killed by culprits such as contradictions, putdowns, dogmatic statements, and gross generalizations. For example:

Don't be ridiculous!
I know exactly what you're thinking!
That will never work!
Are you crazy?
When I was your age, I always. . .
Everybody should. . .
You shouldn't think that way!
How many times have I told you. . .?

Think for a moment about various people in your experience who make conversation difficult. What do they do or say that causes the problem? Is the problem incessant talking? Is it their choice of words, mannerisms, tone of voice, or attitudes that you dislike? It is helpful to make a list of statements and situations that you know are detrimental to dialogue—and then make it a point to avoid each item on the list in your own conversation.

The following questions can start you in the process of detecting conversation killers. Check yourself on each question and take special notice of areas in which you need to improve.

Yes	No	Do I yell or talk too loudly?
Yes	No	Do I complain?
Yes	No	Do I criticize people?
Yes	No	Does the tone of my voice convey disgust?
Yes	No	Do I sound insecure?

Yes	No	Do I talk longer than a minute without giving someone else a chance to speak?
Yes	No	Do I talk about myself or my interests too much?
Yes	No	Do I tend to be dogmatic, condescending, argumentative, or egocentric?
Yes	No	Do I mumble or talk too softly?
Yes	No	Do I have only one topic of conversation?
Yes	No	Do I sound like a drill sergeant—always telling people what to do?
Yes	No	Do I bore people by "talking shop" in the wrong place and at the wrong time?

Asking yourself questions like these can save you from making serious blunders and enable you to make the small adjustments in your speech patterns that are critical to successful conversation.

DEVELOP YOUR THOUGHTS ON INTERESTING TOPICS

Almost any topic is suitable for interesting discussion. Your conversation can be fascinating, whether it's on basketball or jogging, music or politics, door-to-door selling or the stock market. Your thoughts and feeling on any topic are important because they represent *you*. But if this is true, why are so many conversations boring? They probably lack the four essential elements of interesting TALK. First, when our conversations bore others, it is often because we don't *Think* before we speak; we don't consider what will interest the other person. Second, we don't *Assert* ourselves; we don't share our deeper thoughts or feelings, especially when they differ with prevailing opinion. Third, we don't *Listen* intently to what others have said; we miss the clues to deeper meaning that could fire up conversation with warmth, humor, or significance. And fourth, we don't *Know* what to talk about; we don't look for bits of knowledge that can expand our vision of the world or increase our appreciation of the mysteries of the universe—and of each other.

Here are some strategies for injecting into dull dialogues and monotonous monologues some convincing, highly enjoyable TALK:

• When you read a book or magazine, see a movie, or watch TV, search for input that can enrich life, broaden your perspective on issues, increase your awareness of the universe, and sharpen your sensitivity to people.

- Write down or mentally make a note of such input with the conscious goal of sharing it with someone else.
- Start by memorizing small chunks of new information. Even one exciting sentence or thought gleaned from a newspaper, book, or magazine on a regular basis could make you a brilliant conversationalist.
- Treat ideas as potential friends. Don't be afraid of them. Take delight in sharing what you believe is important.
- Learn how to think. Let your mind "wrap around" an idea for consideration instead of automatically casting it into oblivion. Practice looking at an idea or problem from more than one angle: from your angle, of course, but also the angle of someone with a different perspective. Mentally play out an idea to see its short- and long-range consequences.

What will catch your attention might not attract the attention of another. But herein lies the opportunity for sharing your vision of the world, something of the music and beauty, tension and drama within your mind. For example, here are a few thoughts that attracted my attention in just one news article about a seminar for scientists:

> Scientists are trying to discover what happened billions of years ago in the first three seconds of the universe.
>
> They want to know what is gong to happen in the universe in the next 20 to 30 billion years.
>
> They are trying to find one set of rules that will explain both the universe and those particles too small to see.
>
> Seminar participants referred to black holes—collapsed stars so dense that, many theories hold, even light cannot escape their gravitational pull.
>
> Scientists say a teaspoon's worth of black hole could weigh several tons.[2]

When you look for ideas that stimulate your thinking and excite your sense of wonder, you will find them. You will have no trouble sharing them because your enthusiasm will attract and hold the attention of your conversational partner.

LEARN HOW TO ASK QUESTIONS

One of the most neglected skills in interpersonal relationships is the ability to ask good questions. Some think asking questions is a sign of weakness or prying into another's private business. Others concentrate so hard on what they want to say that asking questions never crosses their minds. But people who do practice the art of asking questions generally report three major benefits:

1. Earning the right to be heard.
2. Meeting a need for attention in other people, thus establishing rapport and winning friends.
3. Learning something new.

Some people believe that asking questions is like telling jokes: You either have a knack for it or you don't. The story is told of a new inmate who was eating his first meal in the state penitentiary. Suddenly someone yelled "36!" There were howls of laughter. Then someone shouted "79!" Again the convicts went crazy, some rolling in the aisles with laughter. The new inmate finally asked the fellow next to him what was happening. He replied, "The numbers signify jokes. We've been here so long we just tell 'em by number." Wanting to get along and be accepted, the new inmate mustered his courage a few days later and haltingly called out a number that seemed to be one of their favorites. Nothing. Not even a hint of laughter. A bit shaken, he asked the inmate next to him what happened. The inmate replied, "Some can tell 'em; some can't!"

Some can ask questions; some can't. FALSE. *Anyone* can learn to ask questions effectively. The questions you ask will work best when they reflect your genuine interests and your sense of what is appropriate to the situation. Using the right technique is often critical to getting the response you want.

Here are a few useful techniques to draw upon:

• Recognize that in every encounter there are some emotions involved, perhaps some sense of threat. If you are sensitive to those feelings and seek to reduce the threat by conveying openness and acceptance, your questions will most likely be appreciated.

• Make your purpose clear. Noted pollster George Gallup indicates that when you start asking questions, the other person wonders, "Why does he want to know?" When you state your purpose, even if it's "just for information," you break down the barrier. For example, you might say: "I'm interested in your opinion on a decision I need to make. When will you be free to talk?" or "I'm trying to decide what kind of car to buy. How do you like yours?" or "Honey, our checkbook balance is very low. Do you really want to buy that boat now?"

• Begin your conversation with questions that are easily answered. Then move to open-ended questions that draw out the other person's thoughts and allow him to choose the direction of the conversation. If you want to know the other person's thoughts or feelings on a subject, avoid questions that could be answered "Yes" or "No." For example, instead of asking "Do you like your job?" ask "What do you like or dislike about your job?"

• Listen carefully to how your questions are answered. Check tone of voice, rate of speed at which one answers, what the person actually says, and what the person implies. This information will help you to know how the person is reacting to your questions. Reticence might indicate genuine reluctance to discuss a topic, but often your conversation partner is simply testing you to see if you are really interested. If your partner has been "burned" by persons who ridiculed his deep thoughts and feelings—or simply ignored them—you will need to be patient and first build a relationship of trust.

• Avoid questions that put the respondent in a "hot spot," incite a heated reply, or just "pop" into your head. But keep in mind that most people desperately want someone to pay attention to them, to explore their thoughts and feelings, to inquire about their interests, background, achievements.

MEMORIZE SUREFIRE CONVERSATION STARTERS

Almost without exception, people like to talk about themselves—or anything else, for that matter—if they feel the listener is really interested. Unfortunately, some are so starved for attention that if you give them two minutes they'll take an hour. Yet the possible benefits of asking questions are worth the risk. You earn the right to be heard and you create the most favorable climate for increasing mutual trust and understanding.

Here are a dozen conversation starters to commit to memory. They can break the ice at a party and turn boring "small talk" into satisfying dialogue:

1. If somebody gave you a million dollars, what would you do with it?
2. If you could do any type of work that you wanted, what would it be?
3. If you could be any person whom you know or have read about, in any period of history, who would that be?
4. If someone were to write an epitaph on your gravestone, what do you think it would be? How would you want to be remembered? (Don't start with this one!)
5. What would you like to do or achieve in the next five years?
6. Whom do you admire most?
7. If you won a free ticket to travel anywhere, where would you go?
8. What one achievement do you hope your children will make?
9. Why are you in your business? What keeps you at it?
10. What is most interesting to you about your work?
11. What in life is really important to you?
12. What is your philosophy of life?

In order for these questions to be effective, they must be asked without a hint of a judgmental attitude or the impression that you might misuse the information. Use discretion and your sense of what is appropriate. Add to this list questions related to your own special interests or line of work. Do not contradict or disagree with the answers that you get. You are asking not for scientific fact, but another person's image of his world. The more you convey genuine interest and care about that image, the closer you will come to understanding the fascinating mystery of another human being.

REMEMBER NAMES

More conversations are foiled because of an inability to remember names than there are grains of sand on Newport Beach (well . . . maybe). One's name is a symbolic extension or representation of that person. If you forget a person's name it conveys the message that you don't consider him important. If you want a person to listen to you, you must at least show that person the courtesy of remembering the word more significant to him or her than any other—his or her name!

Often people will excuse themselves by saying: "I remember faces but not names." The folly of this remark is apparent: If you can remember faces, you can remember names. The trick is to connect the face and name in your mind. Here are some suggestions:

1. Listen intently the first time the name is said. Make sure you have heard it correctly.
2. Repeat the name several times in your mind.
3. Use it as often as possible in immediate and subsequent conversation.
4. Cement the name together with the face through association. Look for some outstanding feature of the person's face. Then mentally exaggerate that feature or use your imagination to conjure up some indelible image (the more ridiculous, the better).

This last point deserves further explanation. The key idea here is to change an abstract name (easily forgotten) into an image (easily remembered) that you can *picture in your mind.* Your mind will remember the picture and, by association, the person's name. It will almost be like having the person's name written on his face!

The Memory Book by Harry Lorayne and Jerry Lucas is a fascinating account of how you can make memory systems work for you. Here is an example of how they apply the principle of association to remembering names:

Look, you've just met Mr. Crane. A picture of a large crane, as used by construction workers, comes to mind; or perhaps the storklike bird. You've looked at his face and decided that his high forehead is the outstanding feature. You look at that forehead, and *really* picture many large *cranes* flying out of it; or, you can see them attacking that high forehead! Or perhaps the entire forehead is one gigantic *crane.* As with any association, you have many choices as to the kind of picture you visualize. You must be sure—*force* it at first—to really see that picture. The next time you meet Mr. Crane, *you'll know his name!*[3]

Silly? Of course. But no one else will know about it. With practice, you will find it extremely effective—and fun.

Remembering names can also be profitable. Suppose that in your business you meet five or ten new prospective customers a day. You could jot the name down on paper, use the memory system suggested, review the name and your association a few times, and then put the paper away. You will not forget the name. Just as you feel honored when someone remembers your name, so will your customer when you remember his. Supersuccessful salespeople have mastered the simple procedure of remembering names.

PRACTICE THE SKILLS OF GOOD CONVERSATION

Our minds are constantly churning out ideas or receiving them. Thoughts are forged into words, and on the average we express over six thousand of them in the course of a day. Why then, with such abundant practice, do we not automatically become expert communicators? Practice makes perfect . . . doesn't it? Not necessarily.

If a basketball player does not aim for the basket, his practice shots mean nothing. If a pianist does not use the proper technique, his practice actually could be detrimental. Unless we practice the art of good conversation, we merely develop our propensity for error. Here are eight principles any good conversationalist will practice:

• *Check your attitude.* Are you friendly, cheerful, interested in the other person, flexible, tactful, courteous? None of these characteristics is difficult to develop, yet they comprise the first step toward effective conversation.

• *Relax.* Trying *too* hard and being *too* self-conscious about your mistakes tends to produce a tense atmosphere. People "freeze up" when they don't know what is causing your tenseness, and they become fearful of saying the wrong thing.

• *Think highly of the people you are with.* Even your close friends have faults, but they also have desirable qualities that can be developed. Focus your attention on these qualities. Seek to draw out the best in the people with whom you're talking. This approach can be as contagious as the opposite approach so commonly practiced—that of "finding fault." People generally have an uncanny ability to know what you think of them. If you concentrate on their good qualities, they will be more relaxed and more interested in listening to you and sharing their own feelings.

• *Think highly of yourself.* To do so will not suggest an unhealthy pride or conceit. Rather, it will free you from the burden of self-consciousness so that you may be more aware or conscious of others. If other people detect that you think well of yourself, they will be much more inclined to think in the same way about you.

• *Be alert to the verbal and nonverbal signals you receive from other participants.* Ask yourself: "Am I being heard, understood?" "Am I monopolizing the conversation?" "Are there others who have something to say on the topic?" When the person you are talking to feels that you are not responsive to his signals, dialogue stops. Conversation at its best is a pooling of information, a sharing of interests, a bringing together of ideas from various sources.

• *Keep the long-range goal of your conversation positive.* When a social, business, or personal problem is being discussed, try to come to an agreement on a statement of the problem. (Some people actually do not know what they are arguing about!) When you know what the problem is, you can begin to generate solutions to the problem and keep the conversation from degenerating into nothing but discontent. Although people love to complain, they hate complainers!

• *Think before you speak.* Most problems in communication can be traced to thoughtlessness. Someone said that the trouble with people who talk too fast is that they often say something they haven't thought of yet!

• *Analyze your speech.* Do you pepper your conversation with "um ... ah ... you know"? Does your voice sound pleasing to others? Do the inflection and tone of your voice convey insecurity and timidity, or confidence and authority? Asking yourself questions like these can often provide the awareness necessary to do something about negative speech patterns. But since these patterns frequently are habits, discipline and determination will be required to produce positive changes. A speech teacher or even a friend can be an extremely valuable support in the process of improving one's speech patterns.

The only way to make these principles work successfully for you is to practice them. Practice with total strangers. Practice with business associates. Practice with people closest to you. If you consciously aim to make these principles characteristic of each conversation, you cannot fail to develop the skills of good conversation.

ACTION STEPS
FOR WINNING SELF-DIRECTION

1. From a newspaper or magazine, jot down a few ideas that grab your attention. Commit them to memory and then use them in conversation when appropriate.

2. List several questions that you wish people would ask you. Then ask other people these questions. They will likely return the favor.

3. Use the procedure listed on p. 80 to remember names of people you meet or are introduced to during the week.

4. Make two lists: conversational habits you want to avoid and skills you want to develop. Work on your skills intently for one week and evaluate your progress. Did you avoid some old habits? Did you acquire new skills? Keep going. You can do it!

7

Develop courage to say no

[Children] still cling stubbornly to the idea that the only good
answer is a *yes* answer. This, of course, is the result of their
miseducation, in which "right answers" are the only ones
that pay off.[1]

JOHN HOLT, *How Children Fail*

> An automobile dealer sells the buyer a car he didn't want.
>
> A mother criticizes her forty-year-old daughter's training of her son
> until the daughter gives in to her wishes.
>
> A teenage son ridicules his parents' rules of the house until they let
> him do what he wants.
>
> A male employer offers to promote an attractive young woman in
> exchange for sexual favors. She feels that she has no choice but to
> comply.

Who are these manipulators? They are simply individuals who have learned
that by shouting, pouting, ridiculing, or intimidating, they can force their
victims to give in. All the victims have one thing in common: They don't
know how to say no!

Scientists are now exploring alarming frontiers in mood management, genetic manipulation, subliminal persuasion, and the electrical
stimulation and modification of the brain. As in George Orwell's *1984*,
control technicians seem to be taking advantage of the plasticity of
modern man, molding him to some external specification. A promotional

brochure from one publisher shamelessly claims that their new book reveals how one can totally dominate and control the lives of others and even manipulate their actions as though they were robots! Unless we are on our guard and know how to fight back, we risk being reduced to little more than machines.

This chapter is designed to show you how to fight against external pressure and regain your own internal direction. To achieve control of your life, you will need to know:

Why it is so difficult to say no.
The consequences of saying yes when you want to say no.
How to assert your true self.
Some simple strategies for calmly saying no.
How to say yes to your own life.

A surprising benefit of effectively saying no is increased respect—from both yourself and other people.

WHY IS IT SO DIFFICULT TO SAY NO?

From childhood, many people are conditioned always to say yes. They believe a "yes" response is a *condition* for achieving acceptance. If they try to say no and are rejected, the pattern of saying yes is reinforced and becomes resistant to change.

In a frightening book, *Obedience to Authority*, Dr. Stanley Milgram describes a psychological experiment at Yale University that demonstrates how many people are conditioned to say yes to an authority figure, even to the point of physically injuring another person. Subjects in the experiment were teachers, engineers, salesmen, and laborers. Each experiment involved three people and a "shock machine." One person was the experimenter or authority figure. Another was a "learner." The real subject of the experiment was the "teacher." The shock machine had numerous switches labeled from 15 to 450 volts, and categorized from "Slight Shock" through "Strong Shock" to "Danger: Severe Shock."

The experiment was described to each subject as a study of the learning process. Each subject (teacher) was instructed to read a list of word pairs, such as blue-box, nice-day, wild-duck, and then return to the beginning of the list and say, "Blue—sky, ink, box, or lamp?" The learner was to respond with the proper answer. If he gave a wrong answer—which he did frequently as part of the experiment—the teacher was told to "shock" him. For each incorrect response, the learner would receive a stronger shock—or so the teacher thought (the learners were not actually shocked).

When the teacher objected to increasing the severity of the shocks, the experimenter would reply, "Please go on." If he balked a second time, the experimenter would say, "The experiment requires that you continue." A third objection would elicit "It is absolutely essential that you continue," and a fourth objection drew "You have no choice; you *must* go on." If the subject objected a fifth time, the experiment with that subject was terminated.

What were the results? About two-thirds of the subjects administered what they believed were shocks up to the 450-volt level—even when the learner moaned, screamed, complained of heart pain, and feigned unconsciousness! Why would anyone act so contrary to human decency and common sense? One answer suggested by this experiment is that about two out of three people have been conditioned to fear saying no.

We are born social creatures. Our need for acceptance by others is a built-in need that drives us to social clubs, friendships, even marriage. No one wants to feel rejected, so we tend to go along with the wishes and opinions of others even when we don't want to. The positive side of this tendency is the development of a willingness to compromise to achieve a greater goal and a desire to be responsive to and supportive of others. But when compliance is motivated by a fear of criticism or rejection and becomes so dominant that we reject ourselves and our values in the process, we become enslaved to another person.

Fears about saying no can cause us to be victimized and controlled by others. But they also contribute to a tension within, an identity conflict between two forces that seek to pull the "self" in opposite directions.

THE CONSEQUENCES
OF INTERNAL CONFLICT

Most people love a baby, not because of what he knows or does or says, but because he is "personality plus." There is no facade, no hiding of emotions, no attempt to deceive. In his own way, by crying and cooing, he expresses exactly what he intends. He is spontaneous and responsive to his environment. He is eager to learn and wants to take it all in. He is honest; he is himself. He suffers no identity conflict.

To say no in early childhood was an important part of our identity formation. Our identity formed as we learned to distinguish between ourselves and other objects. For example, the process of learning who we were developed something like this:

No—I'm not that image in the mirror.
No—I'm not the same as my brother or sister.
No—I don't like that food.
No—I don't look exactly like any other child.
No—I don't think the same thoughts or use the same words as someone else.
No—my feelings are not the same as my parents'.
No—I am not this person or that one. I am *me*!

There seems to be a force or desire implanted in our personalities from childhood to be somebody, to be distinct from other people. Unfortunately, there also seems to be a contrary force exerted by society that steers us in the direction of conformity. That contrary force takes the form of certain unwritten social rules like these:

1. People laugh at those who are different—don't let them laugh at you.
2. Make sure your peer group or significant reference group approves of what you do and say.
3. People get hurt feelings or reject you if you disagree with them—so always agree.
4. Security is found in numbers—don't be outstanding.

These rules are often obeyed with an uneasy desperation. People sense that selling out to the crowd means committing treason against the self. Yet social approval is thought necessary for survival.

In a recent study on teenage sexuality, teenagers were asked if they had ever engaged in sexual activities with dates when they really did not want to. Overall, 47 percent of the boys and 65 percent of the girls fifteen to sixteen years old said yes. Among the reason given by girls for acting contrary to their values or feelings were these:

I didn't want to hurt the boy's feelings.
I didn't want him to think I was a prude.
I didn't know how to say no.
I was afraid he would not continue to like me.
I was high on drugs/alcohol.
I felt a sense of obligation.

Boys offered the following reasons:

I didn't want to hurt her feelings.
I was afraid she would think I didn't like her.
I was afraid she would think I wasn't a man.
I did it because she wanted to.
I felt pressure to do it because all my friends were doing it.
I was high on drugs/alcohol.[2]

Daily we are bombarded with hundreds of cultural messages that encourage us to seek approval, to conform—and the messages sink in. When we act on these messages, we become victims of other people's power plays and lose the freedom and exuberance of our true identity. And we lose a degree of happiness.

What brings on our gloom? Is it not a behavior pattern in which we relinquish self-control? For example:

Placating others because one fears offending them.
Allowing others to maneuver one into situations he dislikes.
Always knuckling under to children's demands.
Meekly accepting unjust criticism from a boss or spouse.
Giving in to one's own mental or emotional "demands" to go off his diet, avoid a responsibility, procrastinate.
Exploding with hostility and aggression because one has repressed his real feelings for so long and operated from a position of weakness.

Behavior patterns like these have several unhappy consequences. They lead one into activities that do not express his true self. They distract one from pursuing his own goals. They build resentment and a desire to shy away from people. They limit the number of opportunities for genuine dialogue.

If you consistently say yes when you want to say no, it is important to ask yourself whether a "yes" pattern is worth the subsequent identity conflict and feelings of unhappiness. Ask yourself if a healthy assertiveness would not make you feel better about yourself and even enhance your interpersonal relationships.

ASSERTIVENESS: BECOMING YOUR TRUE SELF

To assert yourself is to positively affirm your true self, to defend your deepest values, to join forces with yourself against your fears and the power plays of others to dictate your behavior. Assertiveness is not aggression. It is not playing the futile game of trying to prove yourself better than someone else. Nor is it trying to gain control over someone. Assertiveness is valuing yourself, acting with confidence, and speaking with authority.

Value Yourself.   To value yourself means to treat yourself as you want others to treat you, respecting the person you are while you nourish the person you want to become. But suppose you feel there are too many things "wrong" with you for you to value yourself? It might be that you are locked into perceiving only those bits of information that you consider negative. For example, some people determine their sense of personal value by:

A parent's harsh word
A dog barking at them
A wrinkle
Clothes that are not the latest fashion
Another's criticism
Lack of money
Intelligence or lack of it
Height, weight, or other physical features
Color of skin
Need for eyeglasses
Age
Past mistakes

> Inability to spell or speak well
> Nationality

When such incidental things affect us deeply, we must realize that we are *choosing* to give meaning to items that many people who value themselves never think about twice.

A striking fact that we learn from studies on information processing is that our eyes are able to see 5 million bits of information per second! But our minds can give meaning "only" to about 500 bits of information per second. Our minds practice *selective perception.*

Perhaps in the past you selected a low value for yourself and consequently became a pawn in other people's hands—but now you want to change that pattern. How do you make that change? By selective perception. Here are techniques that will help you to focus your perceptions in areas that promote positive change.

- Admit that the past is over, that it can no longer rule your thinking and behavior unless you allow it to. Keep in mind that your self-image can be relearned.

- Define the future as wide open—nothing has happened in it yet. No matter how consistently mistakes have occurred in your past, they need not continue in the future.

- Commit yourself to a course of action and conversation that will affirm your unique abilities, values, and beliefs. Say no to all manipulative attempts to control, coerce, and degrade you. Say yes to your need for reasonable freedom. Say yes to your desire to improve yourself—according to *your* standards.

Act with Confidence.   *Confidence* comes from a Latin word which means to "trust." Acting with confidence is trusting the value you have placed upon yourself. It's talking without fear of what others will think. It's saying no when saying yes would be contrary to your true intentions.

How do you gain confidence when you don't really feel it? *Act* as if you have it. Don't worry about whether your feelings support your actions. Begin to take more interest in how you look, what you eat, the fitness of your body. Determine what you think about world conditions. Discover and encourage your best thoughts and most promising personality traits. Concentrate on your strengths. Give yourself a reward for accomplishing even the smallest of goals. Think of yourself as special in all the world. You are!

Acting with confidence can break vicious cycles of fear. For example, suppose you want to suggest a more efficient procedure for handling the paperwork at the office, but are afraid to mention it because the boss does not like people telling him what to do. A fear cycle can be diagramed like this:

1. Bright idea

4. No action

2. Image of boss getting angry at the suggestion

3. Fear

FIGURE 7-1.

Acting with confidence produces a completely different cycle (see Figure 7-2, opposite). Acting with confidence does not imply that you are dishonest or untruthful. It does mean that you choose to override your feelings of fear and assert a behavior consistent with your intentions and will.

Speak with Authority.   A recent study by Duke University anthropologist William O'Barr suggests that people who use a more tentative style of speech are less likely to be believed by a jury. Unconvincing patterns of speech include the following:

You know . . .
Sort of . . .

FIGURE 7-2.

1. Bright idea

4. Action with confidence

2. Development of "soft sell" strategy

3. Image of strategy working

Maybe . . .
Kind of . . .
I guess . . .
Perhaps . . .
Well . . .
I don't know . . .
I think . . .
I wish . . .
Er, uh . . .
Yeah . . .
May I . . . ?
Don't you think . . . ?

Tentative language might be appropriate in some situations. Sometimes the best response is a straightforward "I don't know." However, if you detect uncertain, nonassertive *patterns* in your speech and want to avoid them, create a mental image of yourself speaking with authority. Imagine yourself confidently interacting with people. Select a recent conversation where you backed down or used nonassertive language. What would you have said if you were true to your best self? How would you say it?

If confident speech does not sound "right" at first, try again. Defensive patterns are hard to break. Keep practicing until you feel comfortable with what you want to say and how you say it.

STRATEGIES FOR CALM RESPONSES

If you say no when someone wants you to say yes, there may be conflict. But conflict can be minimized by using the following strategies designed to reduce friction:

• Use the "no sandwich" technique, a negative response sandwiched between two cushioning statements. Since people sometimes associate a "no" with personal rejection, a "no sandwich" can help people "digest" your refusal with minimal negative feeling. It consists of three layers or statements. The first layer is a statement acknowledging what the other person wants you to do. It tells him that you have listened well and understand. The second layer or "meat" of the sandwich is your refusal or the reason why you will not or cannot comply with his wishes. The third layer is something you will do or can say to ease the sting of your refusal. Here are some examples:

1. I understand you want to borrow my car because yours won't start.
2. But I do not let others drive my car.
3. I have some extra time and will be happy to drive you to your appointment.

1. I understand that you want me to agree with you.
2. But I see the issue from a different point of view
3. I hope we can disagree and still be friends.

1. I know you think I should spend more time with your child in his schoolwork.
2. But I have only so much time to give and don't have any more time.

3. Perhaps we could explore the possibility of tutoring. I know an excellent tutor who could help him.

● Keep in mind that an *attitude* of calmness is very important. Anger begets anger, but a calm response turns away anger. If you lose control of your emotions, it is a sure sign that the other person has gained control over you. Say no with quiet firmness, not loud emotionalism.

● If a person persists in trying to control you, use what is called the "broken record" technique. You simply stay relaxed and repeat your refusal in a calm but firm voice until the message gets through.

● Keep in mind that you are nobody's slave. You might need to affirm this truth forcefully to yourself in order to act on it calmly and courageously. But you can refuse to be bound by people who try to intimidate you. You can choose to maintain your inner freedom.

SAYING NO IS NOT ENOUGH

Saying no indiscriminately can become a habit, a trademark, a disavowal of almost everything, a negative mind-set. It can cause you to lose your job or never attempt to find a better one. It can promote disrespect and discord in the home. It can squeeze all the color and joy out of living and bring on despair.

What then distinguishes the positive benefits of a "no" from its destructive uses? How can we decide when saying no is appropriate? These questions are not easily answered. Each expression of "no" requires a personal judgment based on who you are and what you value in life. That is why communication without a system of values is doomed to failure. Without values there is no consistent basis for knowing when to say yes or when to say no, or even what is worth talking about. Furthermore, there is no recognizable foundation upon which to build a bridge of communication with another person. Psychologist Abraham Maslow states:

> The human being needs a framework of values, a philosophy of life, a religion ... to live by and understand by, in about the same sense that he needs sunlight, calcium or love.[3]

One way to sort out and determine your real values is to consider what you would do with your time if you had only three months to live. Whom would you visit? What would you talk about? What changes would you make in your relationships to family, friends, and business associates? What issues would be important? What values that you now hold to be important would fade in significance? If, at the last minute, you were granted another ten or twenty years to live, how would you spend them?

SAY YES TO YOUR LIFE

One person will take from the raw material of life and build a super-structure full of strength, beauty, and sunlight. Another will draw from similar raw materials and build a hovel. In brief, it is possible to take either an affirmative or a negative attitude toward your existence and make of it what you will. To say no to external control is one powerful way of saying yes to your life.

Personal affirmations can be tools for saying yes to your life. In Chapter 3 we discussed how affirmations, stated positively and in the present tense, best help set the mind in the direction you want it to go—even though such affirmations might not yet be presently "true" or realized in your experience. Here are a few affirmations that continue to shape my own life:

I say no to people who try to pressure me in a particular direction against my will.

I say no to my own feelings of intimidation, fear, or worthlessness and refuse to let those feelings control me.

I say no to lifestyles and values that, however popular or tempting they might be, conflict with what I know to be right and true for me.

I say yes to any effort or kindness that enhances the value of other people and myself.

I say yes to a new day of opportunity and challenge—regardless of past mistakes or present obstacles.

I say yes to God, knowing that, as Blaise Pascal said, "Happiness is neither without us nor within us. It is in God, both without us and within us."[4]

ACTION STEPS
FOR WINNING SELF-DIRECTION

1. List the people (spouse, parents, children, etc.) to whom you find it difficult to say no.

2. In a given situation, what would you stand to lose if you said no to the persons you listed? What would you stand to gain?

3. How can taking steps to becoming more assertive benefit you? In what situations (family, social, professional) will you implement these steps?

4. Assuming you really want to say no, write your response to the following persons:

Your teenage child:	"I'm going to take the car to see Tom."
Your spouse:	"Let's invite the Martins over for dinner tomorrow night."
Your boss:	"I want you to have this report ready for me in the morning."
Your mother:	"Don't spank Suzie. She's just expressing herself."
Your friend:	"May I borrow your car for just ten minutes?"

Establish respect when talking with kids

Conversing with children is a unique art with rules and meanings of its own.[1]

HAIM GINOTT

Let's face it. Kids are often too noisy, too forgetful, too unruly, too slow to learn, and sometimes too smart for *our* own good. Yet where kids are there is laughter, learning, growing, reaching for the stars, falling down and trying again—in a word, there is life. And communication with them is a joy when a student says to his teacher, "I really learned something today," or when a daughter tries to console her mother during a difficulty with a tearful "I love you, Mom," or a son concludes a conversation with "Dad, you're my best friend."

No more awesome responsibility can be undertaken than to train a child. Often we fail. None of us has a total grasp in every situation of all the complexities of a child's physical, mental, emotional, social, and spiritual development. Although we can't be perfect at relating to children, we can be adequate.

Mutual respect is the basis for adequate relationships. When respect is clearly evident, then the foundations are established for increasing the quality and, yes, even the joy of talking with kids. This chapter focuses on seven foundational principles designed to enhance and convey mutual RESPECT:

R — Remember your childhood
E — Encourage self-esteem
S — Stop hassles before they start
P — Practice behavior you expect
E — Elicit your child's "world"
C — Communicate love
T — Transfer significant values

REMEMBER YOUR CHILDHOOD

What were you like as a child? What made you happy? What made you angry? What adult did you respect the most or have the most fun with? Why did you enjoy that person's company? How can you be more like that person now in relating to your children?

If talking with children is not a joy, it might be that you have neglected the answers to these questions. It happens to all of us. Perhaps that's why the article "Father Forgets" by W. Livingston Larned hit a nerve in America many years ago and has become a classic piece of journalism throughout the world:

> Listen, son: I am saying this as you lie asleep, one little paw crumpled under your cheek and the blond curls stickily wet on your damp forehead. I have stolen into your room alone. Just a few minutes ago, as I sat reading my paper in the library, a stifling wave of remorse swept over me. Guiltily I came to your bedside.
>
> These are the things I was thinking, son: I had been cross to you. I scolded you as you were dressing for school because you gave your face merely a dab with a towel. I took you to task for not cleaning your shoes. I called out angrily when you threw some of your things on the floor.
>
> At breakfast I found fault, too. You spilled things. You gulped down your food. You put your elbows on the table. You spread butter too thick on your bread. And as you started off to play and I made for my train, you turned and waved a hand and called, "Good-bye, Daddy!" and I frowned, and said in reply, "Hold your shoulders back!"

Do you remember, later, when I was reading in the library, how you came in, timidly, with a sort of hurt look in your eyes? When I glanced up over my paper, impatient at the interruption, you hesitated at the door. "What is it you want?" I snapped.

You said nothing, but ran across in one tempestuous plunge, and threw your arms around my neck and kissed me, and your small arms tightened with an affection that God had set blooming in your heart and which even neglect could not wither. And then you were gone, pattering up the stairs.

Well, son, it was shortly afterwards that my paper slipped from my hands and a terrible sickening fear came over me. What has habit been doing to me? The habit of finding fault, of reprimanding—this was my reward to you for being a boy. It was not that I did not love you; it was that I expected too much of youth. I was measuring you by the yardstick of my own years. . . .

It is a feeble atonement: I know you would not understand these things if I told them to you during your waking hours. But tomorrow I will be a real daddy.[2]

From our own reservoir of knowledge based on our childhood experience, we can recreate an image of what it means to be a child, how it feels to think and act like a child. When we have that image clearly in mind, we can develop a basis for understanding children today. Of course, the times are different. Certain customs and attitudes are gone and new ones have taken their place. But underlying all the changes are some fundamental needs in children that are likely never to change. If we can put ourselves in touch with our own childhood, we prepare ourselves to meet those needs. We take the first giant step toward experiencing the joy of talking with children.

ENCOURAGE SELF-ESTEEM

When a child does not feel good about himself, it is likely he will not feel good about what people say to him. He may interpret innocent remarks as threats or condemnations. He may talk back in anger and frustration because one of his most basic human needs has not been met—a sense of personal worth. Whether we call this need self-appreciation, self-love, self-celebration, or self-esteem, one thing is sure: It cannot be constantly frustrated without serious consequences to one's personality and expression of himself. Children often do not have the psychological defense mechanisms and recovery strategies that enable adults to cover up or heal the hurt of blows to their self-esteem.

Self-esteem does not come easily for children, especially in a society infatuated with superior intellect, beauty, and skills. The subtle but powerful message of the social environment is that if you are not outstanding, you are not worth much. Unfortunately, adults sometimes convey this same message to their children. They communicate acceptance on the basis of their children's *performance* rather than their *being.* In attempts to improve performance or change behavior in children, adults sometimes say:

You will never amount to anything!
You never do anything right!
You got passed over when the brains were passed out!
With grades like that, you'll turn out to be a bum!
You can forget about football; you'll never make it!
Your dog is smarter than you are!
You're a naughty boy!

A very bright but troubled fifth-grader explained to me that he couldn't do the work in school. When I asked him why, he said: "Because my mother always says that I can't do anything right." He believed her.

Normally, communication problems with children are not the result of a lack of love, but a lack of sensitivity and training. Although it is true that parents are sometimes blamed instead of trained, many do remarkably well with limited knowledge. But in the area of identity formation, there is one profound psychological truth every parent and teacher ought to know well. S. I. Hayakawa puts it simply: *"What you tell a child he is, he will become."*[3] In other words, children tend to become what they are told they are, even if that identity is negative! The psychological need for an identity—any identity—is greater than the child's readiness to evaluate the information he receives. Thus, if a child is told he is a "crybaby" or "bad boy," he will believe that is how he should act. Conversely, if a child is told that he has a good mind and can solve problems, he will think of himself as a problem solver and learn to use his mind creatively.

Most of us want our children to feel good about themselves and have a positive, realistic attitude about their capabilities. Often we know how to generate these kinds of attitudes. But we don't always act on our best knowledge. We fall prey to the frustrations of the moment. Unconsciously we develop communication patterns contrary to our deepest values and cherished hopes for our children.

To assess whether you encourage self-esteem in your children, ask yourself four basic questions:

1. *Do I listen intently to my children?*   Self-esteem is generated in children when we listen, deeply listen, to them. Yet after a hard day of work, a parent is often drained of patience and the desire to understand. Parents have a right to relax a bit with a newspaper or TV. They need periods of peace and quiet to get recharged. But sometimes these "periods" last indefinitely and a child's attempts to talk are constantly rebuffed.

One evening a young boy tried to show a scratch on his finger to his father. After repeated attempts to gain his father's attention, the father slammed his paper down in his lap and yelled in exasperation, "Well I can't do anything about it, can I?" Fighting back his tears the boy replied, "Yes, Daddy, you could have looked at it and said 'Oh.'"

Perhaps we are too busy. A study by Cornell psychologist Urie Bronfenbrenner showed that fathers spend on the average only 37.7 *seconds* a day in any meaningful conversation with their children. If we do not reserve time to listen, then one day, when we are ready to listen, our children might not have time to talk.

2. *Do I show respect for my children?*   Examine your *attitudes* about your children. Do you believe the old saying "Children are to be seen, but not heard," or do their thoughts and feelings deeply matter to you? Do you believe that children are barriers to your own personal advancement or do you believe that they are a treasured responsibility and present a most awesome challenge for your own development?

Some parents are ambivalent about these questions. Some feel one way but convey a contrary attitude. To clarify ambivalent feelings that you might have, ask yourself these questions: What attitude do I want to have toward my children? Do I convey that attitude or some other? Do my children know I respect them?

Psychologist Eric Fromm sees respect as a major component of love. In *The Art of Loving*, he writes:

> Respect is not fear and awe; it denotes, in accordance with the root of the word (respicere—to look at), the ability to see a person as he is, to be aware of his unique individuality.[4]

Respect also means having faith in the potential of the other person. Think about the powerful boost in life you would receive as a child if an adult significant to you conveyed to you this kind of respect.

3. *Do I cultivate a positive mental attitude in my child?*   The proverb is true for children, too: "As a man thinketh, so is he." Children become what they think about most. Children with feelings of inferiority may perpetuate their own problem by dwelling on negative characteristics and thus developing self-fulfilling prophecies. For example, an overweight child might say:

> I'm always hungry.
> I'm too clumsy to play baseball.
> I can't stop eating.
> No one will ever choose me for the team.

Self-criticism in children can become a bad habit. It accomplishes nothing except depression or resignation to a low-level existence—never trying, never risking, never winning.

One of the greatest discoveries of our time is that people can change through self-conditioning. Just as children can make themselves literally sick by worry, so they can make themselves healthy by focusing on their best qualities. But they need positive input to do this.

You can teach your children a "no-knock" policy—a refusal to concentrate on negative qualities in themselves or others and a determination to accentuate the positive. One fifth-grade teacher in California consistently had the top performing class in school, regardless of whether she was given bright or hard-to-teach students. She had the fewest discipline problems, and among the student body her class always showed the highest morale. When the principal asked her for an explanation, she admitted that she religiously kept a daily record of whom she complimented and how often. She never dismissed the class until each student had received at least one genuine compliment.

4. *Do I encourage my children to develop their skills and talents?*   Some parents misunderstand the nature of encouragement. One mother thinks she is encouraging her teenage son by paying all his bills. Another constantly answers for her son when he is asked a question. But encourage-

ment is not overprotection or shielding a child from life's demands. These actions discourage because they communicate a lack of trust in the child's ability to handle the situation.

Encouragement is aiding the development of courage. It is saying to your children:

I like the way you solved that problem.
You are learning to control your anger.
I see improvement in your ability to dribble the basketball.
This math is difficult. I'm proud that you solved so many problems correctly.

On the other hand, do not exaggerate. If mother says, "You're a genius" when the child has only half of his homework correct, the child will think: "If this is genius work, I can get by with a lot less effort."

Honestly encourage by commenting on achievements, even small ones, already accomplished. Encourage by an attitude of support and confidence in the child as he faces new challenges. Encourage by being ready to show acceptance and love for your child even when he fails, because you hold his worth and value constant in your mind by virtue of his being, not his performance.

A famous pianist was scheduled to give a performance in a stylish London concert hall. About a half-hour before the famous performer was expected, the hall was already packed with dignitaries in formal dress. On the bare platform, spotlights focused on a very large grand piano. One admiring mother had taken her seven-year-old son because she hoped he would practice with more enthusiasm if only he could hear a great pianist.

In the noise of conversation, the young lad quietly slipped out of his seat. His mother soon noticed that he was missing and began looking frantically about the packed auditorium. Then she heard a very familiar sound drift out over the suddenly hushed crowd. Her eyes flashed to the piano where she spotted her son sitting on the bench prepared for the master. With the spotlights on him, he played "Chopsticks"!

"Chopsticks!" someone yelled in anger. "Get that kid down!" The embarrassed mother was so busy working her way through the crowd that she did not see the internationally famous pianist slip prematurely onto the stage and sit beside her son.

"Chopsticks" remained very clear in the music that followed. Everyone could hear "Chopsticks." But the master pianist started to fill in all around the simple tune. He played spine-tingling runs and made the makeshift piano duet into a masterpiece. When the mother was close enough to the stage, she heard the master encouraging her son, "Keep going, boy. Don't stop now. I'll help you. You've got it. Keep going!"

STOP HASSLES
BEFORE THEY START

According to *Webster's New World Dictionary*, the word *hassle* was coined in America. Perhaps Americans wanted to describe a situation somewhere between "haggle" and "tussle." At any rate, every child and adult knows exactly what hassles are and what they feel like. Especially bothersome are recurring hassles about bedtime, eating, TV viewing, chores, homework, who should be first, and who owns what. They are common enough that many take them lightly. But constant hassle is abrasive and takes the joy out of communication.

Can hassles be avoided? Yes! Since hassles require two or more participants, you can simply refuse to play the hassle game. Instead, you can establish the ground rules for resolving a disagreement. For example:

> Johnny, I will not argue with you. I will not shout at you and I do not expect you to shout at me. I will hear you out and try to understand you. And I want you to try to understand me.

What has the adult done? He has established a clear set of rules for discussion and let the child know he wants to understand. Of course, this approach is only the beginning in solving certain problems. But it prevents talk from becoming a bitter "haggle" or "tussle."

Some strategies for ending hassles take an authoritarian approach—a rigid emphasis on absolute control by use of force. But force is a poor motivator. It does not produce lasting change. Consequently, force tends to escalate, resulting in verbal and/or physical abuse. At the other extreme is the permissive approach—letting a child say or do whatever he wants. But children tend to push the limits of acceptability, often verbally and emotionally abusing the adult. Neither approach avoids hassles, but rather generates them.

I recommend an authoritative approach that combines high control with positive encouragement. It avoids the pitfalls of the permissive and authoritarian approaches and provides the most effective way to avoid hassles. The following five strategies are the ABC's of an authoritative approach to hassle-free communication with children:

A – Analyze problem behavior
B – Be clear about your expectations
C – Catch them doing good
D – Discipline in love
E – Exert your authority firmly, but calmly

Analyze Problem Behavior.   Hassle from a child might be caused by frustration, disappointment, a sense of rejection, a feeling of not being loved, or a defiant spirit. It is necessary to determine the true cause of a behavior. Otherwise wrong solutions will be applied to the problems—and the hassle will continue.

Suppose your child consistently is late in getting off to school. Every morning it's the same story: hassle and nagging resulting in unhappiness for you and the child. When the child finally does leave for school, he's mad at the world and in no mood to learn anything. Notice how the parent in the following dialogue does not falsely presume to know the cause of the problem (such as laziness), but uses active listening to discover the real source of the problem:

Parent: Son, you are consistently late for school. What are you feeling? What is the problem?
Child: I don't like school!
Parent: You don't like school?
Child: It's boring!
Parent: You feel you already know what the teacher is teaching?
Child: Well, no, but it's not important.
Parent: You feel it doesn't relate to you.
Child: Right. What does subtracting fractions have to do with me? Why do I have to learn that stuff?
Parent: You feel it's hard to learn and you want to know why it's worth it.
Child: It is hard to learn. A lot of kids are having problems with fractions.
Parent: You feel bad when you don't understand what's happening.
Child: Yes! I feel stupid! *(Begins to cry).*
Parent: I see. *(Silence. Puts arm around son. . .)*

Parents and teachers who are most successful in communicating with children will try to look at a problem from the child's point of view as well as their own. This does not mean approval. But it provides the adult with information on how to help the child face his problem and overcome it.

In trying to assess the cause(s) of problem behavior, the adult should keep the following questions in mind:

What is the real problem?
Have I contributed to the problem by my tone of voice or accusing remarks?
Does my child understand what I expect?
How have I tried to handle this situation before?
Was it effective?
How can I best handle this situation now?

Be Clear About Your Expectations. Children make assumptions about what adults expect of them. Sometimes the assumptions are distorted or completely wrong. This dialogue shows how that problem can be corrected.

Parent: It's hard to want to go to school when you have those feelings.
Child: (Silence.)
Parent: What can we do about it?
Child: You can stop demanding that I get all A's like Susan!
Parent: Do I demand that?
Child: Well . . . you are always telling me how good she is in math.
Parent: Son, listen carefully to me. I don't demand any particular grades from you in any subject. I just want you to try hard and do your best.
Child: (Silence.)
Parent: You want to know something?
Child: What?
Parent: I did not get good grades in math either when I was your age.
Child: Really?
Parent: Yes. Let's work on the math together and see what we can learn.
Child: OK.

In this example, the child is motivated to do the work because the burden of feeling compared to Susan (and constantly losing) has been lifted and his parent's expectations clarified. Keep in mind that an adult's expectations for a child have not been adequately communicated by an adult until the child fully understands them and can repeat them in his own words. Thus, it is helpful to ask a child: "What do I expect you to do?"

Take a positive approach to the tasks you want your children to do. Write down routine expectations and chores and go over them with the child until he is able to satisfactorily repeat what is expected. This will eliminate the retort "I didn't know you wanted me to do that!"

Catch Them Doing Good. Express delight at a chore accomplished. Compliment children on work well done. Psychological studies show that positive reinforcement is more effective in shaping behavior than criticism. One study by David Rosenthall, a professor of psychology at Harvard University, asked the question: "What would happen to a group of children of standard mental ability if their teachers were told that the children were actually 'late bloomers' and would tend to manifest a great increase in intellectual achievement throughout the coming year?" The results of the experiment showed that those identified as "late bloomers" did increase their intellectual performance on tests significantly more than others. Rosenthall interpreted this result as indicating that communicating positive expectations to children can positively influence their behavior.

An observing parent will find opportunities during the day to make such comments as:

I like the way you come for dinner when you are called.
I appreciate your hanging up your clothes even though you were in a hurry to play.
Thanks for telling me the truth about what happened.

Keep in mind that unless praise is sincere, the child will soon view it as meaningless. Excessive praise also loses its effect. But genuine compliments motivate positive change and reduce hassle.

Discipline in Love. The word *discipline* has been used to describe everything from beatings to bribings. When hassle becomes intolerable, adults often "discipline" their children with the same ambiguity—with no clear concept of what, why, or when to discipline. The result is that what they call discipline is ineptly delivered and ineffective.

Discipline which produces long-lasting, positive results is discipline with love. Such discipline may include imposing restrictions, enforcing limits, and spanking, but it is always administered in harmony with the attitude of love—a firm, tough love which maintains boundaries for behavior—but still love.

A helpful distinction can be made between this new approach to discipline and old patterns of punishment. In *Help, I'm a Parent*, psychologist Bruce Narramore diagrams the differences this way:[5]

	Punishment	Discipline
Purpose:	1. Inflict a penalty	1. Train for correction
Focus:	2. Past misdeeds	2. Future correct deeds
Parents' Attitude:	3. Anger and frustration	3. Love and concern
Resulting Emotion in Child:	4. Fear and guilt	4. Security

The consistent exercise of this kind of discipline will minimize hassles. In the following example, notice that there is an absence of anger and frustration and the presence of discipline for the future:

Parent: Son, what are you supposed to be doing?
Child: Feeding the dog.
Parent: What *are* you doing?
Child: Nothing.
Parent: You know what the consequence is for not doing the chores in the time we agreed on?
Child: Yes, Dad. No TV tonight.
Parent: The purpose of that restriction is to help you remember next time and keep your mind on what you're supposed to be doing.

If an adult loves a child, he will discipline him. His action will communicate to the child that he is an ally in the struggle to control negative impulses. It says that he cares enough about the child and himself to set boundaries and take the time to enforce them for the long-range benefit of both child and adult.

Exert Your Authority Firmly, but Calmly. Some people feel that their authority increases with the volume of their voice. I heard about a schoolteacher who had a terrible problem controlling her class. Whenever she got really angry, she would jump up on top of her desk and blow a whistle at the kids. The kids loved it! During recess and lunch they would plot how to get another "command performance" started again.

By contrast, my son's fifth-grade teacher exercises a very powerful, silent authority in his class. He simply employs a stern stare at a misbehaving child. If that does not immediately bring the child within the limit, he gives the child a task, such as writing fifty "rules." Every child knows that writing rules is a logical consequence of misbehavior. The teacher seldom needs to raise his voice. His authority is respected and admired by the class.

There is a time when talk must stop and *action* must communicate your authority. However, it is action, not anger, that motivates the desired response in the child. If you tend to delay disciplinary action until you are upset or angry, you are waiting too long. You can act sooner without anger. When you act before you lose control of your emotions, you gain greater authority and save yourself unnecessary stress. The key to exerting your authority firmly but calmly is acting before your emotions sabotage your authority and ability to act wisely.

The ABC's of hassle-free communication are not difficult. But if you are not now using them, you will need to commit yourself to mastering a new approach. Power struggles should be avoided whenever possible. But those times when they are inevitable, when the child's behavior is defiant, the parent needs to win and win decisively. If the parent can maintain calmness in the process of dialogue and discipline, he stands the best chance of increasing the child's respect for him and of avoiding the alienating force of anger.

PRACTICE BEHAVIOR YOU EXPECT

Think about this question for a minute: Are your own conversation patterns really consistent with the kind of conversation you expect from your children? I am convinced that most parents and teachers want the best for their children. When conversations fail, the cause often is not the absence of goodwill, but the failure to apply one's own values to one's conversations.

Writing down a "communication code" for yourself is an excellent way of gaining consistency between your communication patterns and your values. It keeps you on track. It helps you to act on what really is important to you in talking with your children. When writing your own code, ask yourself these two basic questions:

1. What do I want to accomplish through my communication with children?
2. What is the best way to proceed toward that goal?

Some goals worth considering are:

> Develop mutual respect.
> View matters from the child's point of view as well as my own.
> Sense what a problem feels like to the child.
> Show forgiveness.
> Convey love.
> Build self-esteem.
> Develop a healthy sense of humor.
> Promote internal discipline.
> Aim for cooperation.
> Achieve understanding.

Once your goals are formulated, you will need to develop effective strategies to reach them. Be careful not to be deceived. Methods that seem to "get results" can be counterproductive in the long run. For example, the following practices create distance and defensiveness:

> Screaming, yelling, threatening, bribing, name-calling, crying, pleading, sarcasm, teasing, ridiculing, insulting, interrupting.

Although these efforts might bring about temporary compliance, they do not teach or demonstrate respect. If a child experiences disrespect, he tends to react as an adult would—with resentment, bitterness, and a desire for revenge. Moreover, children mirror the strategies of their parents and teachers. If father yells, the child will learn to yell. If mother screams insults, the child will learn the same. If a teacher uses sarcasm, so will the child. The pattern follows naturally the law of reciprocity: What you hear is what you say.

ELICIT YOUR CHILD'S "WORLD"

What is your child's "world" like? What does he think about, feel or imagine? What's funny to him and what does he wonder about?

Young children see the world differently than adults do. To their uncluttered minds, the world is not bound by laws of gravity, cause and effect, or space and time. They can fly to the stars, walk on planets, win fierce battles against evil giants and slay monsters. When their imaginations are nurtured, their conversations are blessed with creativity, drama, emotion, trust, and a capacity for wonder. From his wide experience with children, Dr. Benjamin Spock claims:

> One of the most delightful aspects of children is the originality of the things they say, especially during preschool years. Their remarks, their ways of interpreting things, are usually fresher, more vivid even than those of great philosophers and writers. Yet lots of parents never think of paying attention to these gems of perceptiveness.[6]

Some parents complain, "My son is like a stranger to me. He won't tell me what he's thinking," or, "I never know how my daughter really feels about anything. When I ask her, she shrugs her shoulders and says she doesn't know." Why do children keep their "world" hidden? One common cause (discussed in Chapter 2) is the fear of being judged or evaluated negatively. Parents tend to evaluate what a child says by adult standards rather than enjoying a conversation by the child's standards. For example, if a child reports that he killed a huge monster last night, the parent can choose to respond with "That's silly, there are no monsters" or "Wow! That must have taken a great deal of courage!"

Children can destroy one another's dreams, too. When Lucy pleads with Charlies Brown to tell her his dream and then laughs him to scorn for wanting to be called "Flash," it is reasonable to conclude that Charlie Brown will not quickly share his dreams again. The real tragedy is that a child might not only stop sharing his dream, but stop dreaming, or begin to scorn his "world" as others seem to do. The tragedy is what dies inside a child while he lives.

Adults can reverse this tendency and help children to appreciate one another's "world" for what it is. They can gently probe a child's "world" with questions and then enjoy the answers. They can enter into a spirit of joint exploration at the child's level. They can choose not to impose adult "correctives" such as "That's not possible" or "When will you ever learn to face reality?"

When I was in college I did not appreciate a child's "world." I was shocked when my professor in a child psychology class reported how he set aside a half-hour each day to enter as fully as he could into the "world" of his children and experience it with them. If they wanted to play "Monkey" or "Kangaroo," he would pretend to be that animal. To Dr. Brown, the experience that mattered was the extreme delight of his kids. When they finished playing, they could talk about anything. The children knew their dad could understand them and wanted to. He had proved it.

Children desperately want to be understood. To understand them, explore their thoughts and feelings by asking questions, lots of them. But do not ask questions that make them defensive or uneasy. Make a list of questions you want to discuss just for fun or mutual benefit. Ask open-ended questions that require your child's input rather than "yes" and "no" questions. Here are several to help you get started with your list:

What do you like to dream about?
What do you think makes the book we are reading so interesting?
Just for fun, how do you think the earth got here?
Why did you like that science-fiction movie so much?
If you didn't need to worry about your clothes getting wet, how do you think you would feel walking in the rain? What does rain feel like?
What person outside of our family do you admire most? Why?
What would you like to be when you grow up? What kind of work do you think would be most interesting?
When do you feel like laughing . . . or crying?
What is it like to be a fifth-grader in your school?

Eric Fromm in his book *The Art of Loving* writes about a child's need to receive "milk" and "honey" from his parents. "Milk" refers to meeting a child's physical needs. But "honey" is the added touch of flavor, the special attention, the sharing of experience that produces the sweetness of life. Reading good books with your children is a rich source of "honey." It's a great way to share the adventure of life together, to discuss questions as they arise, to feel the failures and successes of book characters and to learn from them. Books can spark a child's curiosity and fan into flame his capacity to wonder, to savor life in all of its goodness and fullness. They can expand a child's world and bring him out of his introspection. They can provide a common meeting ground between your world and his.

COMMUNICATE LOVE

Some people believe that if they love a child, the child will feel loved. Not necessarily. Dr. Alice Ginott states:

> It is our incompetence in communicating love, *not* our lack of love that drives children crazy. Most of us love our children. What we lack is a language that conveys love, that mirrors our delight—and that makes a child feel loved, respected and appreciated.[7]

Children seem to be concerned about two basic questions: "Am I loved?" and "How much can I get away with?" Sometimes a parent falsely assumes that to maintain behavior control, he needs to keep the child wondering about his first question. If he uses name-calling or subtle putdowns to keep a child in his place, he is replacing a language of love with a language of unacceptance.

Language of unacceptance is heavy in evaluation, judgment, criticizing, and moralizing. Suppose a child is building a castle in the sand. Language of unacceptance would include the following:

> That's not how sand castles look!
> Here, let daddy help you do it right.
> Don't step on it, stupid!
> You can do better than that!
> Why are you just sitting there? I thought you wanted to build a sand castle.

It is a misconception to think that language that shows acceptance of a child will be interpreted by the child as acceptance of negative behavior. And it is a misconception to think that nagging will produce positive change. A major principle that we learn from clinical counseling is that when a person feels he is truly accepted by another as he is, then he feels free to move forward in his personal development. He is motivated to think about how he wants to change and become more of what he is capable of being.

A language of love conveys acceptance of the child. It will include firmness and limits, but it will communicate these unmistakable messages to the child.

> You are loved.
> You're OK.
> You're accepted
> You're forgiven.
> You can try again.

A language of love is not just calling your child "Champ," "Buddy," or "Princess." Rather, it is a part of the whole system and quality of your communication.

Especially for children, nonverbal communication can be a language of love more important than words. Perhaps because of their limited vocabulary, children are very sensitive to voice tone, facial expressions, and the attitudes that our behavior suggests to them.

Touching is a language of love. Many studies of children and infants show that few things are more important to early physical and mental growth than touching. Children and infants deprived of physical contact suffer greater learning difficulties and emotional adjustments than those who have experienced adequate body contact. The evidence is overwhelming. Touching conveys caring. Even a genuine pat on the back is vital. A hug, a kiss, a tap on the arm, holding hands, assisting when needed—these all are ways of communicating love in language the child understands best—action language.

A study of the mothers of fifty prominent Americans and how they brought up their children showed that love and support of their children were common characteristics. However, there is a fine line between showing an interest in a child and taking over his life, between supporting and overprotecting. These mothers clearly knew the difference. While they lavished love on the children, they also required the children to do for themselves whatever they could.

Communicating love is not always easy, especially if parents are threatened or feel judged by the behavior of their children. Parents sometimes wonder, "What will Aunt Sally think of me when she sees Mike act like this?" Does it really matter? Do we want to allow other people to come between us and our children? Unfortunately, children do not understand these social complexities. They simply ask: "Am I loved?"

TRANSFER SIGNIFICANT VALUES

Parents ask: "How can I teach my values to my children? How can I compete with some of the values being taught to my children by music, movies, magazines, and TV?"

We need to get back to the basics. You can learn what is most important to you by determining which of your values are most enduring. Try writing them down. Decide which of the values you listed correspond to your children's current physical, mental, social, and spiritual needs. Then don't hesitate to express your values. Competition from outside influence will be tough. But if you develop a relationship with your children of open, frank communication, if they know that they can trust your values because they see them demonstrated, if they know you really care about them—then you have more than a fighting chance.

Search for opportunities to share your values in a natural, appropriate way. But then seize the opportunity. Young people have confided to me that they really don't know how their parents feel about premarital sex or using drugs. They are not sure what really is important in their parents' lives or in their own. Their parents have never discussed these topics with them.

Such a knowledge vacuum about significant values is dangerous. It opens the floodgates for any system of values from any source. Some 2400 years ago, Plato asked rhetorically: "Shall we just carelessly allow children to hear any casual tales which may be devised by casual persons, and to receive in their minds ideas for the most part the very opposite of those we should wish them to have when they are grown up?"[8]

In a study that compared American and Soviet children, Urie Bronfenbrenner reported on the TV viewing of children in the United States:

By the time the average child is sixteen, he has watched from 12,000 to 15,000 hours of television. In other words, he has spent the equivalent of 15-20 solid months, 24 hours a day, before a television screen. . . . It would be folly to *ignore* the possible effects and to allow this massive intrusion into the daily lives of children without at least questioning its impact.[9]

Let's not leave the value development in our children to sources that could undermine the very values we believe in. Let's not shy away from discussing our values with our children because we don't have time or we feel embarrassment.

When my son reached the age of ten, I said something like this to him:

> Jud, in a few short years you will experience a strange new world called adolescence. It can be a wild and confusing time or it can be an exciting adventure in growth. The key is preparation. In order to start preparing for it, how would you like to go on a camping trip over the weekend—just the two of us? We'll call it your "pre-adolescent trip." When Jessica gets to be your age, she can have her own "preadolescent trip" with Mom. You and I can plan where we want to go and what we want to do. And as we go, you can ask me any questions you want and I'll try to answer them. I'll share some things I've learned along the way, too, that will help to make adolescence an adventure.

As a springboard for discussion we used an excellent cassette program developed by Dr. James Dobson entitled *Preparing for Adolescence*. We discussed how to avoid the "Canyon of Inferiority" and how to be prepared for the physical changes and emotional pressures that would occur during adolescence. In the process I shared to the best of my ability the values that I believe enrich life and lead to enduring happiness.

Do not be surprised or intimidated when you discover that other parents and their children do not have the same values you do. Allow for differences without defensiveness. Occasionally review your values, upgrade them perhaps, but do not change them simply because some "authority" or a certain number of people have a different set. Know how your values compare with those to which your children are exposed. Develop confidence in values you hold and think about why you hold them. Then share those reasons with courage and enthusiasm.

Children desperately want to know what the limits are morally, as well as what principles give you joy and fulfillment in life. Such knowledge will help them to carve out their identity with boldness and security. They will know who they are, in all their uniqueness, because you have communicated well who you are.

Values are internalized when they have been fully accepted as one's own, both emotionally and intellectually. If children, and especially teen-agers, are to internalize values, they need freedom to test their wings, to make mistakes, to be forgiven, to start over again. As the child grows older he should gradually and on an increasing scale be given as much responsibility for his own actions as he can handle. Of course, the transfer of values is never smooth or simple. But when even small steps are taken, parents can take delight in one of their greatest accomplishments—aiding the process of children becoming mature, fully functioning, value-directed adults.

The Reverend Jesse Jackson tells black teenagers, "You can't plant the seed and pick the fruit the next morning."[10] Good communication with children doesn't happen overnight either. First, you plant the seeds of communication awareness within the nutritious soil of your love. You add the sunlight of new conversational skills and the water of refreshing attitudes. Then time is required—time for pulling out the weeds of poor habits and time for growth. In due time, both you and the children in your care will enjoy the fruit.

ACTION STEPS
FOR WINNING SELF-DIRECTION

1. How would you rate yourself on the following questions? Circle the number that best represents the frequency (1 = low, 4 = high) that each item occurs in your experience.

1 2 3 4   I listen intently to my children.

1 2 3 4   I show respect to my children.

1 2 3 4   I cultivate positive mental attitudes in my children.

1 2 3 4   I encourage my children to develop their skills and talents.

1 2 3 4   I analyze problem behavior.

1 2 3 4   I make clear my expectations.

1 2 3 4   I catch my children doing good.

1 2 3 4   I discipline in love.

1 2 3 4   I exert my authority firmly, but calmly.

1 2 3 4   I have long-range goals for the moral development of my children.

1 2 3 4   I'm happy with my progress toward these goals.

1 2 3 4   I use strategies designed to help me reach my goals for my children.

1 2 3 4   I seek to enter into my children's "world" in my conversations with them.

1 2 3 4   I search for opportunities to share my values with my children.

Does your self-evaluation suggest areas in which you need to improve?

2. In this chapter, I discussed seven foundational principles for establishing respect between adults and children. What two or three principles are most pertinent to your situation?

3. Concentrating on the principles you selected, what are some specific actions you intend to take? (For example: "I will make the tone of my voice affirming, not judgmental or harsh.")

Create closeness
with people
you care about

> "We glide past each other . . . because we never dare to give ourselves."[1]

DAG HAMMARSKJOLD

In the hospital corridor a young man cried softly. Not until his father died did he learn from his mother how much his father had loved him. Of course, the young man was expected to have known, somehow. But the real hurt now was the realization that he knew his father better at the moment of his death than he did when he was alive. During his life the barriers had been kept too high, the distance too great.

Intimacy means "within." It refers to a relationship that allows another person to cross the normal boundaries of defensiveness and enter into that space where we are most truly ourselves. Although most of us desperately want intimacy, at the same time we fear it.

The risk in intimate communication is that the other might not accept us after we have shared our deepest feelings. But the alternative is aloneness—the failure to know another's love or deep respect even when it does exist.

Communication is the key to intimacy, for it is only through the exchange of meaning and the sharing of feelings that deep understanding and psychological closeness can be achieved. Of course, the meaning shared is of a special kind. Intimate communication occurs when a friend opens his heart to you in such a way that you are encouraged to come out from behind your mask and into a fresh experience of mutual understanding. In that experience you are more open, more ready for positive growth, more loving, more alive.

Intimacy is not necessarily sexual. In fact, sexual relationships might not be intimate at all except in a purely physical sense. Intimacy can exist between parents and children, husband and wife, brothers and sisters. It is experienced among friends, relatives, even business partners. When intimacy develops, we experience a sense of relatedness, belonging, and acceptance that is extremely satisfying.

WHY INTIMACY
IS SO CRUCIAL TODAY

Parents, family, friends—what would our relationships be without them? How crucial is our support of one another, how necessary to our mutual happiness that we share the pain and joys of life together, how vital the smile, the phone call, the kiss, and those words without price, "I love you!"

Intimate relationships are our means of transcending ourselves, of breaking out of the loneliness and ugliness of the egocentered prison. When we come to a loved one's deathbed, then we know intuitively that things do not matter, people do. We know that although ambition, success, and the pursuit of excellence are high values, the greatest of all values is love. Love builds up the other person as well as ourselves. For these reasons, people hunger for love.

When we feel physically hungry, we simply take action to satisfy our physical need. The "hungers of the heart" are more complex to satisfy. We can exist without these needs being met. Yet we can know the depths of human joy only when the hunger for love is fulfilled.

WHY INTIMACY
IS SO HARD TO FIND

Listen to one married couple tell their stories.

Mike: I'm intimidated by Susan. She's beautiful and I'm so lucky to have her. But I don't know how to talk to her. I love her and try to show it in many ways. When I putter around the garage or fix things in the house, it's because I love her. I built this house for her because I love her. I bought her an expensive coat and ring because I love her. I will do anything to make her proud of me. The real questions are, "Does she love *me*?" "Will *she* try to put our marriage back together?"

Susan: We have not communicated well for ten years. It's not just one thing, but many things. We have built a wall between us, one brick at a time. That's why I've been meeting Roger. He knows what I feel. I can tell him anything and he understands. Mike never had any sisters. He doesn't know what women feel or what they like. He doesn't touch me affectionately or seem interested in really understanding me. He seems to be married to his work. Although he wants sex, our sex life is not good. We don't have a common outlook. We don't feel a unity.

If our desire for intimacy is motivated by an inner need to love and be loved, why is intimacy so difficult to achieve? Why do people misinterpret the basic signals of the heart? Why are our real intentions so often camouflaged or distorted?

Susan mentioned that she and Mike had built a wall between them one brick at a time. If we are to experience intimacy, we need to look at these "bricks" that eventually create barriers. We need to know how and why the barriers are built in order to gain the inner strength and courage to break them down and make them unnecessary.

The first brick is *fear*. Mike never revealed who he really was to Susan because he was afraid of her reaction. He was afraid that his weaknesses and faults would be discovered. That kind of fear is a barrier to intimacy, an enemy of love. Afraid to let our defenses down, often we communicate on the surface and with thousands of devious disguises of our true feelings. We isolate and insulate ourselves so as not to become too vulnerable. In fact, by these actions, we actually pursue loneliness.

A second brick, closely related to the first, is *insecurity*. Because Susan did not sufficiently assure Mike that he was loved, he began to doubt his own lovableness. Insecure and defensive, he developed self-protective games, or what psychoanalyst Harry Stack Sullivan called "security operations." He became "married" to his work. His will to relate and desire to love operated under heavily guarded conditions. The thought and energy expended to protect his fragile ego prevented its strengthening through genuine contact and honest interaction.

A third brick that builds a wall between a couple is a *focus on being loved.* Because Susan was so intent on being loved her way, she missed the hundreds of ways Mike tried to show his love. She was not free to help him express his love in mutually acceptable ways. She became resentful that her needs were not being met and bitter as she counted all her grievances.

A fourth brick is *game playing.* In interpersonal transactions, games are substitutes for intimacy. They include ulterior motives and manipulation patterns. Susan's affair with Roger is an example of the game "You Hurt Me, So I'll Hurt You." Some games provide mutually accepted patterns for dealing with frustration, aggression, and even the desire for closeness. But deep down each partner knows the games are not the real thing. Manipulating, hiding, and emotional distance go together. The games are maintained because of the fear of real intimacy and mutual transparency.

A fifth brick is *repressed emotions.* Repression is the process by which we hide our emotions not only from others, but ourselves as well. We repress emotions because they tend to be so powerful, so often misunderstood, so elusive of the control of reason.

About nine-tenths of an iceberg remains submerged. A similar ratio has been suggested in regard to emotions. The emotions we communicate are a fraction of our total feelings. We are unaware of our hidden emotions much of the time and thus are baffled when the intensity of some feeling surfaces. In one counseling session, Mike indicated that he was beginning to feel emotion for the first time, but didn't know how to express it because he had repressed it for so long.

A woman related to me how she had expressed some deep emotion to a small group of friends she thought she could trust. But the expression of that emotion caused a subtle chain reaction of events that eventually led to recrimination and deeply hurt feelings. Concluded the woman: "I will never share my deep feelings again."

But repression is not the answer. It attempts to deliver to a "dungeon" that which is the deepest, strongest, most colorful part of the self. In spite of the risks, the honest expression of emotion can bring about personal and interpersonal growth. The repression of emotion is likely to bring stagnation in relationships . . . or decay.

A sixth brick is *fatigue.* Mike never showed Susan his best self. In the morning he was in a rush to get to work. In the evening, he worked at odd jobs about the house. When he finally went to bed, he was exhausted. In Susan's words, Mike was a "workaholic."

When a person experiences fatigue, his mind and body are intent on self-preservation, on conserving what little energy is left. He is not able to listen well or share deeply.

A seventh brick is *time pressure.* Often we hear someone say, "I don't have time to talk about that now." Pressured by a hundred and one things we think we need to do, we cut out the joy of intimacy. We treat intimacy as a luxury, a quality to cultivate when we "have time." Of course, we will never have time unless we make time to develop the kind of relationships we really want with each other.

TEN COMMITMENTS FOR A CLOSE FRIENDSHIP

Barriers to intimacy can be dismantled the same way they are built—one brick at a time. But to remove barriers and build bridges, commitment is necessary. Commitment connects you to your goal of intimacy. It alerts your mind to think according to your plan, it directs your behavior to be consistent with your intentions, it keeps your communication on track.

Commitment is a personal matter. Reading the following commitments will not do a thing for you unless you choose to make them your own. Further, intimacy, like all effective communication, is a two-way street. If the other person does not care about you, intimacy will not occur. But caring is related to knowing, and knowing is related to sharing, and sharing yourself well is something you can do. If you choose to make the following commitments a part of your plan, you are on your way toward sharpening your interpersonal skills and creating closeness:

1. *I will be a friend.* If you want to have a friend, be one. Think about all the qualities you want in a friend. List them on paper. Ask yourself which of those qualities you need to work on. Then commit yourself to improving those qualities.

2. *I will make the satisfaction, security, and development of my friend as significant to me as my own.* This is an adaptation of Harry Stack Sullivan's classic definition of how love acts. It has dynamite power in destroying barriers and creative power in building togetherness. It is the best way to be a best friend.

3. *I will make time for togetherness.* One study shows that married couples spend, on the average, only 27.5 minutes out of every 24 hours

talking to each other, but more than 6 hours per day watching TV. Love needs time to act. Friendships need time to develop. Emotions need time to become clear and be expressed. Thoughts need time to be collected, sifted, organized, and articulated. Time is necessary to express thoughts and feelings that are consistent with one's real intentions.

4. *I will celebrate the uniqueness of my friend.* A true friendship encourages each one to be himself, to be free, to be different. Resist the drive to create a replica of yourself for the sake of security or for any other reason. Be patient regarding all that is unresolved both in yourself and in the other. View differences as a challenge to your verbal skill at achieving cooperation. Develop the attitude that differences in those close to you are complements that add to, rather than detract from, your identity. Encourage differences in others that represent worthy values and you will at the same time be drawing out the best in yourself.

5. *I will avoid criticising, condemning, and judging the other person.* This attitude is sensible and necessary because none of us is perfect. The "law of mutual exchange" is clear: If you judge others, you too will be judged. Keep clearly in mind the distinction between a person and his action. You can support the *person* even when you cannot condone his *actions.* This distinction will be conveyed in the tone of your voice and your body signals. An attitude of personal support also provides the best climate for negative behavior to be transformed. It motivates positive change.

6. *I will initiate compliments.* When two people have limited inner resources of self-esteem to draw on in a crisis, cycles of mutual retaliation often develop and whirl on with increasing momentum. The "mutual exchange principle" here proceeds like this: "If you hurt my feelings, I'll hurt yours. If you say mean things to me, I'll say them back to you." Practice since childhood makes us experts in using this principle. But the mutual exchange principle can work just as effectively in positive interaction as it does in retaliation. Compliments are strongly evident in healthy marriages and friendships. Each is motivated by the exchange principle to draw out the best in the other.

Complimentary exchanges don't continue effortlessly. Stress, frustration, overwork, time pressure, fatigue—and perhaps a hundred other daily pressures—do their work in breaking the flow of positive statements. Someone must take the initiative, break the deadlock of silence, and squelch a cycle of retaliation.

Initiatives such as the following often have a simplicity that belies their power to gradually narrow emotional distance and produce an interlocking of personalities. For example:

"I like the way you think."
"I like the way I feel when I'm with you."
"You make my day."
"Your friendship is valuable to me."
"You light up my life."

7. *I will listen for and respond to feelings as well as thoughts.* Clinical experience shows that when feelings receive special attention without judgment, they are powerful motivating factors for stimulating conversation. So listen for feelings . . . feelings of hurt or failure, but also feelings of optimism and victory. When a husband relates that he gave his best report ever to the board, the wife could say, "Wow! That must have felt really good!" instead of "Will they give you that raise now?" Listen for feeling words. Untangling the logic, clarifying the facts, moving on to discuss your thoughts—all that can come later. If you do not pick up on feelings when they come, the rest of your conversation will be next to meaningless. Feelings expressed in close relationships are almost always more important than the thoughts that surround them. Zero in on the feeling . . . and your friend will know you as a friend.

8. *I will seek not so much to be understood as to understand.* To *understand* means to stand on the same "ground" where the other person is standing. It means to "walk in the other person's shoes," to see reality through his or her eyes. We can never understand another perfectly because reality is always perceived by our own unique framework for making sense of it. But we can come close. For the moment we can disengage our minds from our own interpretations and try to see an issue from the other's viewpoint.

Each moment of conversation requires new effort. Understanding in past moments helps, but it does not automatically extend into the present. Because thoughts and feelings change constantly, a concentrated, determined effort to listen actively is necessary in each new conversation.

9. *I will fight for intimacy.* When most fights occur, the pattern is too familiar: two different worlds of thought and feeling colliding, then an explosion of hostile words or actions, followed by hurt feelings and psy-

chological distance. But there *is* a style of fighting that results finally in intimacy rather than distance, a fight that both partners can win. For this kind of fight, there are only three rules.

a. Yelling, insults, lies, deceit, name-calling, and bringing up mistakes are all "below-the-belt" and must be avoided.

b. Each participant must verbally reflect the other's feelings about a point, *to that person's satisfaction,* before arguing his own point. For example, a husband might say: "You feel embarrassed that I made such a fool of myself at the party last night." The wife then accepts or corrects that interpretation and the husband goes on to make his point.

c. The goal of the fight is understood to be intimacy, understanding, and closeness—not distance, competition, or winning at the expense of the other.

What a difference following these three simple rules could make in our fighting! Of course, there might be hurt feelings, defensiveness, insecurity, anger, a need to change behavior. But the really damaging punches would be eliminated. Each would be forced to listen deeply to the other. Both would be fighting to get back on the same wavelength, to reach the same goal. How could anyone lose in a fight like this?

10. *I will ask the greatest healing question.* There is one question that, when asked in all sincerity, produces miraculous healing in relationships. Some people seem to have trouble asking it because they grew up with the idea that they always had to be right. They believe, probably unconsciously, that to be proven wrong on some point of thought or behavior is an indictment against their very *self*—not just an indictment against some perception or action. They seem not to have built up a generalized sense of worth.

But when one grows out of such ridiculous notions, when one becomes convinced that his personal value will remain even if he admits a mistake, then he can ask this healing question—"Will you forgive me for what I've done, for my contribution to our problem?" Mountains of bitterness can melt in a moment. A thousand-mile gap of psychological distance can be closed in a second. Skeptical? Check with couples and families where the question is asked. Analyze relationships where forgiveness is practiced. You will find miraculous healing.

When I ask the question, I am not assuming all blame. I am not deciding who was "right" and who was "wrong." Blame is never that one-sided. "It takes two to tangle." But the question communicates: "I acknowledge my part in the problem. I am asking you to take me back into your love from which I feel separated."

When a genuine friendship develops, what happens? Each partner is willing to talk freely and listen deeply. Even small, insignificant bits of information are gladly, eagerly received. In the process, something happens. Respect, self-worth, positive perspectives blossom. For troubled marriages, too, intimate communication provides the best possible chance for a rebirth of vitality, adventure, and love.

Intimate communication is a peak experience. The cumulative effect of intimate conversations will always be profound, always issuing in a greater vitality, self-esteem, and desire to participate in the enrichment of others' lives. Problems viewed in the process of peak communication are less imposing, solutions more accessible. In dialogue at this level you are encouraged to step out of the shadows and into the sunshine, out of the coldness of isolated thoughts and into the warmth and fun of having your thoughts fit those of another.

EXERCISES FOR
INTIMATE COMMUNICATION

The following questions get to the heart of our thoughts and feelings. They will encourage intimate conversation if you ask them in love and listen in love. Timing is important. Choose an appropriate time with your spouse, family members, or friends. Don't hurry through all these questions at one time. Concentrate on the questions that seem most intriguing, or make up your own list of questions. Approach each conversation as an opportunity for creating closeness.

What makes you happy?
What do you feel anxious about?
When do you feel most secure?
When do you feel most alone?

What do you think is the most critical problem in our relationship?

If you were sure you could not fail, what would you attempt to do?

If you could live your life over, how would you choose to make it different?

What qualities do you look for in a friend?

If you had one month to live, how would you choose to spend the time?

What gives you a feeling of hope?

What would have to happen for you to feel really fulfilled?

How can we reach our realistic goals together?

ACTION STEPS
FOR WINNING SELF-DIRECTION

1. With your spouse or close friend, share your thoughts about the seven "bricks" discussed in this chapter that create barriers between people. For example, which bricks are most troublesome in your relationships? How did they get there? How can you eliminate them?

2. Avoid speaking only about the problems in your relationship. Also share some of the vitality and the reasons that you are attracted to each other.

3. Tell your conversational partner of your commitment to a positive, mutually satisfying relationship. Use the strengths in your relationship and the "Ten Commitments for a Close Friendship" to reach your relationship goals. Keep choosing manageable-sized goals—steps you can take in the next twenty-four hours to increase understanding and create closeness.

4. From the section "Exercises for Intimate Communication," select three or four questions from the list of questions that you and your partner want to focus on and write your answers on a piece of paper. Thousands of couples in marriage encounter seminars have found that exchanging written answers adds a surprisingly helpful dimension to their communication. You will, too.

10

Dissolve discord

Experience convinces me that the *number* of conflicts in groups
(including families) is not at all indicative of how healthy they are.
The true index is whether the conflicts get resolved and by what
method they get resolved.[1]

THOMAS GORDON, *Leadership Effectiveness Training*

Two psychiatrists arrived at the same elevator at the same time. Their
offices were on the third and tenth floors, respectively. When the elevator
reached the third floor, the first psychiatrist turned to the second, spit in
his face, and strode off the elevator. The second psychiatrist never changed
his demeanor. He simply took out his handkerchief and wiped his face dry.
Dumbfounded, the elevator operator asked: "Why did he spit in your
face?" The psychiatrist thought for a moment, shook his head, and said:
"I don't know. Anyway, it's his problem, not mine."

That's *one* way to respond to interpersonal tension—but there must
be a better way! This chapter focuses on how to dissolve discord between
you and another person before it begins to feel like spit on your face.

Some conflict between people is not only inevitable, it is healthy.
Absence of conflict can be a sign of indifference, which may be the worst
of our human failings. But honest expression of differences can move a
relationship from insensitivity to new understanding. Of course, healthy

tension does not always bring agreement, but eventually it leads to workable solutions and seeks the resolution of hostility.

In contrast, unhealthy tension is characterized by continuing discord—the bickering, the ongoing argument, the fighting over even insignificant details, the sulking silence. Discord drives people apart. It interferes with reasoning and destroys the desire to understand. If interpersonal relationships are to be meaningful, we must find ways to dissolve discord.

REASONS PEOPLE FIGHT

What causes discord between people? This question is a tricky one because what we think is a cause might, on further investigation, turn out to be merely a symptom of a deeper cause. Yet the question is useful. It can help us gain insight about why we sometimes engage in verbal fights and it can alert us to problem areas that we need to work on.

The following items provide a quick checklist of common causes of discord. Keep in mind that continuing discord may have multiple causes. For each of the following items that seems relevant to your situation, indicate by circling the appropriate letter whether that item affects you (Y), your spouse (S), your children (C), or some other person (O) important to you (e.g., a friend, business associate, neighbor):

Causes of Discord	You	Spouse	Child	Other
1. Stressful environment	Y	S	C	O
2. Fatigue	Y	S	C	O
3. Time pressures	Y	S	C	O
4. Financial worries	Y	S	C	O
5. Different belief systems	Y	S	C	O
6. Contradictions	Y	S	C	O
7. Dishonesty, lying	Y	S	C	O
8. Criticism	Y	S	C	O
9. Parental interference	Y	S	C	O
10. Sibling rivalry	Y	S	C	O
11. Business or career decisions	Y	S	C	O

Causes of Discord	You	Spouse	Child	Other
12. Housekeeping chores	Y	S	C	O
13. Lack of self-esteem	Y	S	C	O
14. Uncaring attitudes	Y	S	C	O
15. Selfishness	Y	S	C	O
16. Moodiness	Y	S	C	O
17. Insecurity	Y	S	C	O
18. Mid-life crisis	Y	S	C	O
19. Sexual concerns	Y	S	C	O
20. Invalid assumptions	Y	S	C	O

Continuing discord might not be caused by external factors, but by internal tensions. Typically, persons with internal tensions experience fatigue because of the great energy spent in attempting to reconcile divergent desires. Fatigue, in turn, increases edginess and decreases willingness to make the effort to understand. Often persons with internal tensions will try to prove that they are not responsible for the discord. For example:

Why pick on me? What did I do?
It's not my fault—it's yours!
Why did you get us into such a mess?

People suffering internal tensions will produce discord everywhere they turn until they assume responsibility for resolving their personal problems. They may need professional help. But often they can solve the battle within by talking openly with conversational partners who will listen nonjudgmentally.

HOW TO GET BACK
ON SPEAKING TERMS

Once discord has set in, talk is difficult. In fact, discord may have resulted from talk—from sharing hostile feelings or dogmatic opinions. Yet talk also can be the best remedy when it is directed by four distinct purposes and their corresponding messages:

Purpose	*Message*
1. Define the problem	("I hear . . .")
2. Look for agreement	("I agree . . .")
3. Understand feelings	("I understand . . .")
4. State views calmly	("I think . . .")

These four steps provide a simple but powerful model for *conflict resolution* (CR). This CR model can help you get back on speaking terms with your conversational partner.

To use the CR model, first *define the problem.* Do you and your partner really know what the issue is? Are you both talking about the same thing? Semanticist S.I. Hayakawa illustrates the snowballing effect of mistaken assumptions:

> We have all had the experience of being at meetings or at social gatherings at which Mr. X says something, and Mr. Y believes Mr. X to have said something quite different and argues against what he believes Mr. X to have said. Then Mr. X, not understanding Mr. Y's objections (which may be legitimate objections to what Mr. X didn't say), defends his original statement with further statements. These further statements, interpreted by Mr. Y in the light of mistaken assumptions, lead to further mistaken assumptions, which in turn induce in Mr. X mistaken assumptions about Mr. Y. In a matter of minutes, the discussion is a dozen miles away from the original topic.[2]

Avoid mistaken assumptions by saying "I hear you saying that. . . ." Refuse to proceed with the discussion until you have stated the point to your partner's satisfaction.

Second, *look for agreement.* There must be something in your partner's viewpoint with which you can agree—some detail or obvious bit of truth. Say "I agree that . . ." and then focus on details about which you both can honestly agree. For example:

> I agree that I said some unkind things.
> I agree that we are both tired.
> I agree that your brother meant well.
> I agree that I have made the same mistake.

This step will require active listening on your part—and that is part of its power. Plus, it's positive. You are looking for areas of *agreement*. When you find viewpoints that you both share, you cause the other person to relax because the argument is a bit less threatening. Consequently your partner reduces the threatening nature of his talk and you begin a mutual relaxation of tensions. "I agree" messages narrow the subject matter about which you disagree. They can take the sting out of the discussion and set the stage for talking a conflict through to its resolution.

Third, *understand feelings*. Few things are more important or more powerful in an argument than your partner's feelings. Say "I understand that you might feel. . . ." and then complete this sentence with *one* word that describes what you think your partner is feeling. Use a word that describes a feeling, not a thought or behavior. For example, you might use one of the following:

angry	troubled
depressed	upset
defensive	uncertain
hurt	revengeful
worried	elated
anxious	happy
afraid	confident

Tendering your perception of the other's feelings shows that you want to understand. If you misinterpret the correct feeling, your partner will tell you. When you state it accurately, you establish one additional powerful source for dissolving discord because most people desperately want to be understood at the level of their feelings.

Fourth, *state your views calmly*. Say "I think . . ." or "The way I see it is . . . ," and then as calmly and briefly as possible state your opinion. For example:

I think that you ignored our prior agreement.
I think that you are drinking too much.
I think that I need fifteen uninterrupted minutes to relax when I come home from work.
I think that my study comes first; play time comes after that.

You will need to decide whether you are serious about breaking the discord pattern. If you are, avoid name-calling, putdowns, and judgmental evaluations. Yelling and screaming are weak, childish reactions to the tensions of the moment. Choose to speak firmly, but without raising your voice. Choose to reduce the sense of threat, because although threatening talk might "win" the argument temporarily, it does not dissolve discord.

Dissolving discord produces dramatic changes in one's interpersonal relationships. In the midst of discord, individuals speak *at* each other, missing each other's points and generating more heat than light. But when the conflict resolution model is employed, the focus of the controversy gradually changes from attacking one another to attacking a mutual problem and solving it. We can diagram it as shown on the opposite page.

As the shift in focus occurs, there is a corresponding change in the interpersonal relationship.

1. Individuals speak *with*, not *at*, each other.
2. They are less defensive and more open.
3. They are less angry and achieve greater understanding.

In the following sections of this chapter, we will apply the four-step conflict resolution model to marital, parent-child and business relationships. In each example, compare the discord exchanges with dialogue that uses the CR model to bring about resolution.

TALKING YOUR WAY OUT OF MARITAL TROUBLE

> *PROBLEM AREA: FINANCES*
> *Husband:* Look at this checkbook!
> You didn't balance it again
> and now we're overdrawn!
> I suppose you like paying
> five-dollar fines! How
> stupid can you get?

Discord Exchange	*Resolution Exchange*
Wife: You don't always balance either! Why are you yelling at me?	*Wife:* (Step 1) I hear you saying that you are angry at me for my mistake. Is that really the problem?

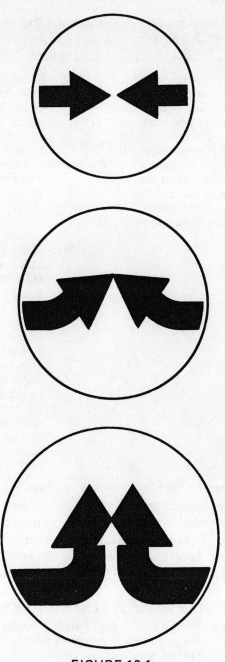

FIGURE 10-1.

Husband: Because when we are overdrawn, it's always you who messed up somewhere.

Wife: So you think you're perfect? The last time we had to pay a fine it was because you were speeding in a residential area. Thirty-five dollars!

Husband: What about the time you hit the side of the house with the car? Three hundred and eighty-five bucks down the drain!

Husband: Well, we try so hard to save, but it seems we never can save enough.

Wife: (Step 2) I agree that it is hard for us to save. Everything costs so much. We certainly don't need extra expenses like fines.

Husband: I'm afraid that we're not going to have the money we need for that ski trip we've dreamed about.

Wife: (Step 3) I understand that you might be frustrated.

Husband: I really am!

Wife: (Step 4) I think that I need to do a better job of recording the checks. But more than that, I think we need to work out a better system for keeping track of what we spend and for setting aside more for the trip. I'm willing to work on it with you.

Comment: The "Discord Exchange" is now far from the real cause of the tension and is likely to continue with mutual recriminations. The "Resolution Exchange" uncovered a major frustration in the husband. His initial outburst was triggered only incidentally by the overdraft fine. Now that the real concern has been brought out into the open, there is a good chance the husband and wife can solve the problem together.

PROBLEM AREA: SEXUAL CONCERNS

Wife: What do you think I am? A machine? Do you think if you push the right button, you'll get an automatic response?

Discord Exchange	*Resolution Exchange*
Husband: There is no response. You're not a machine. You're an iceberg!	**Husband:** (Step 1) I hear you saying that something I do makes you think I want a certain kind of response.
Wife: You're not so hot in bed either! Remember what happened last week?	**Wife:** Yes. I guess I feel that our sex has gotten to be kind of mechanical . . . just going through the motions.
Husband: Do you blame me? Who wants to make love to an iceberg?	**Husband:** (Step 2) I agree it seems that way at times. (Step 3) And I understand that you might feel used.
	Wife: Yes, I do.
	Husband: (Step 4) I think that we need to talk more about how we feel and what we want from each other. Sometimes I feel used by you in some ways. I think neither of us wants that kind of relationship.

Comment: Most "sexual problems" are not truly sexual problems, but result from discord in the relationship. Discord is built on a judgmental, demeaning, hostile spirit. Resolution is built on an open, nondefensive, caring spirit. There is a good chance that the husband in the Resolution Exchange will win the communication game because he's helping his wife to win, too.

PROBLEM AREA: MID-LIFE CRISIS

Wife: Our life isn't going anywhere.
The fun and excitement are gone.
Here we are—almost 45—and what
do we have to show for it?

Discord Exchange	*Resolution Exchange*
Husband: Get off it! You've got a new house. I bought you a car last year. What the heck are you complaining about?	**Husband:** (Step 1) I hear you saying that it seems like we're on a treadmill.

Wife: Well, Susan. . .

Husband: Susan! All you talk about is Susan! You think she's got it better than you, right? She doesn't even own her home. You know what your problem is. You're going through your change of life already!

Wife: *(Begins silent anger treatment.)*

Wife: Yes, especially when I look at Susan's life.

Husband: (Step 2) I agree that Susan seems to be happy. What is it about Susan's life that you like?

Wife: Susan is so confident of herself. She is growing as a person.

Husband: (Step 3) I understand how a person might feel depressed when making a comparison with someone who seems so self-assured.

Wife: I don't think she's more talented than I am. I don't feel worthless or inadequate. But she's making progress toward what she really wants in life. I don't even know what I want anymore.

Husband: (Step 4) I think we need to investigate this problem more before we can solve it. What do you think about inviting Susan and her husband over for dinner? We could ask them what their secret is.

Comment: Tension exists in our lives for a reason. It can produce destructive discord; or, if one chooses, it can serve as a catalyst for highly productive talk. The exchanges above show the difference between defensive, judgmental, angry talk and talk that seeks to reduce threat and demonstrates a willingness to explore creative solutions.

Believe that you can talk your way out of marital trouble! Perhaps you won't see much progress in your first attempts. But if you consistently employ the principles of the CR model, you stand the best chance of influencing your marital partner to walk the same path with you—and talk along the way.

REDUCING FAMILY TENSIONS

PROBLEM AREA: SIBLING RIVALRY

Jim: (a child) to Carl (another child):
Your nose is too long, your ears
are too big, and you smell like
the garbage can!

Discord Exchange

Parent: Shut up! What are you, some kind of nut? You don't talk to your brother that way!

Jim: Why are you always yelling at me? You should have heard what Blabbermouth said about me!

Parent: I don't want to hear it. You kids are driving me crazy. Both of you go to your room!

Jim and Carl: But. . .

Parent: Shut up! Go.

Jim: But it was his fault!

Carl: I didn't do anything wrong!

Resolution Exchange

Parent: (Step 1) Jim, I hear you saying some very unkind things. What seems to be the problem?

Jim: Carl called me a weakling on the school bus—in front of everybody!

Parent: Carl, what happened?

Carl: But he couldn't even open the window. . .

Jim: It was stuck!

Parent: Jim, how do you feel about what happened?

Jim: Angry! I felt that Carl was making fun of me.

Carl: I didn't mean anything by it. . .

Parent: How many times do I have to tell you?!?

Parent: (Step 2) I agree that you may not have meant anything by it, Carl, and (Step 3) I understand that you might feel angry, Jim. (Step 4) I think that you need to apologize, Carl, and both of you should be more sensitive to how each other might feel next time.

Comment: In discord exchanges, there is no resolution. While the command "Shut up! Go to your room!" might seem to get rid of the tension, it merely covers it up temporarily. The angry feelings between Jim and Carl remain strong. Furthermore, the parent is now angry at both of them. Angry feelings in each of the three persons involved in the discord likely will surface again at the slightest provocation.

In the "Resolution Exchange," the parent acts as a facilitator by helping Jim express his true feelings and helping Carl to understand them and take responsibility for reconciliation.

PROBLEM AREA: DEFIANT BEHAVIOR

Child: I will not go to bed at nine o'clock! None of my friends do!

Discord Exchange

Parent: When I was your age, I had to go to bed at eight-thirty.

Child: But that's old-fashioned. No one my age would go to bed at eight-thirty or even nine.

Parent: I don't care what you think! Please do what I say.

Resolution Exchange

Parent: (Step 1) I hear you saying that you don't want to go to bed now because your friends don't go to bed at this hour.

Child: That's right!

Parent: (Step 2) I agree that your friends may go to bed later than you do. (Step 3) And I understand that you might feel angry that we have a different schedule.

(Step 4) But I <u>think</u> you
need to realize that we
don't set our time
schedule by what other
people do. In ten minutes
it will be nine o'clock. I
expect you to be in bed in
ten minutes.

Comment: Defiance in children is part of the growing-up process. It's one way children hammer out their identity against the anvil of parental authority. But parents need to recognize that they can exercise authority most effectively when they are loving but firm. Halting speech will be viewed by the child as weakness or indecision and a great opportunity to battle against the parent. Pleading and arguing are not effective. Calm but decisive talk and action are effective.

MANAGING CONFLICT ON THE JOB

PROBLEM AREA: CONTRADICTION
Roger: You don't know what you're
talking about!

Discord Exchange

Pete: Look, I've studied this
problem. I know I'm right.
This is the only way we can
solve our production
problem.

Roger: It is not! How many
times do I have to tell
you—it won't work. I've
been here longer than you
have. I ought to know.
etc.

Resolution Exchange

Pete: (Step 1) I <u>hear</u> you saying
that you <u>think</u> I'm wrong.
(Step 2) I <u>agree</u> that I
might be.

Roger: Well, I suppose I could
be wrong, too.

Pete: (Step 3) I <u>understand</u> that
you might feel anxious
about solving our
production problem.

Roger: Yes, I am.

Pete: (Step 4) I think we need to review both your proposal and mine. Together I think we can take care of the problem.

Comment: Direct contradiction is one of the most common causes of discord. It causes the other person to defend himself and try to "save face." In the "Resolution Exchange," Pete defused Roger's anger by admitting that he might be mistaken and by listening to Roger's ideas. The result was a focus on solving the problem together—not on who had the "correct" perspective.

PROBLEM AREA: CONFRONTATION

Employee: You're always checking on me!

Discord Exchange

Manager: Right! And you know what I find? I'll tell you: extended coffee breaks, lousy attitudes, and sloppy work.

Employee: I know some facts about you: a two-hour lunch break last week! And three weeks ago you forgot that appointment with Mr. Douglas. That probably cost the company hundreds of dollars.

Manager: You're fired!

Resolution Exchange

Manager: (Step 1) I hear you saying that you don't want me to check on you.

Employee: Exactly!

Manager: (Step 2) I agree that you might not like my checking on you. (Step 3) And I understand that you might feel uncomfortable when I do check on you.

Employee: You haven't heard the end of this!

Employee: It does make me feel uncomfortable. I feel that you think I'm not doing an adequate job.

Manager: Are you?

Employee: No.

Manager: Why not?

Employee: I've been having severe headaches for about a month.

Manager: I'm sorry, Tom. What do you plan to do about it?

Employee: I should see my doctor, I guess. But I keep putting it off.

Manager: (Step 4) Tom, I think that you need to see your doctor as soon as possible. We care about you and we want to keep you here. But we need to see some specific improvement in your attitudes, time management, and quality of work. Are you willing to see your doctor and begin improving in these areas?

Employee: Yes.

Comment. In the "Discord Exchange," the manager comes on unnecessarily strong. He provokes the employee to anger and retaliation without ever discovering the real problem. In the "Resolution Exchange," Steps 1, 2, and 3 reduce the employee's defensiveness. As a result of the employee's openness, the manager senses there is more to the problem than just laziness. He returns to defining the problem and uncovers a significant reason for poor work. He shows personal interest in the employee's health and yet makes his point effectively regarding the employee's improvement.

In applying the conflict resolution model to various areas of tension, we have seen certain common elements in both the "Discord Exchange" and "Resolution Exchange." The following chart summarizes what to avoid and what to practice when you face conflict:

Discord/Resolution Chart

DISCORD PRODUCER	CONFLICT RESOLVER
1. Immediately assumes he knows what the problem is	1. Takes the time to discover and define the real problem
2. Tries to gain upper hand and prove his correctness	2. Looks for areas of agreement to reduce threat and signal a desire to resolve the conflict
3. Talks—doesn't listen	3. Listens actively to understand how the other person feels
4. Allows choices and actions to be dominated by feelings	4. States his viewpoints calmly, but firmly

In the past few years, we have seen the rise of discord in the home as well as between groups of people. One similarity among those who promote discord is their self-serving and narrow-minded attitudes. By their strident demands, they damage not only their personal relationships, but sooner or later they must damage larger public values. This chapter is a call for a basic spirit of accommodation and mutual respect that will promote not only the resolution of conflict, but the enhancement of everyone's self-interest.

ACTION STEPS
FOR WINNING SELF-DIRECTION

1. Describe an unresolved conflict you are experiencing (as you see it) in each of the following areas:

a. Marital partner   _____

b. Children   _____

c. Business associate _____

2. Try to describe the same conflict from the other person's point of view:

a. Marital partner   _____

b. Children   _____

c. Business associate _____

3. For one or more of the conflicts you listed above, write out a "Resolution Exchange" as you imagine it would develop if you used the conflict resolution (CR) expressions "I hear . . . ," "I agree . . . ," "I understand that you might feel . . . ," and "I think. . . ."

4. Now use the CR model in actually talking with these persons. Make any necessary adjustments in your approach and try again. Record the results below:

a. Marital partner   _____

b. Children   _____

c. Business associate _____

Persuade people to cooperate with you

Influencing people is the art of letting them have your way.

ANONYMOUS

As I write this chapter, my eleven-year-old son Judson is preparing to ride his unicycle in his first parade. I'm proud of his achievement. Almost anyone can ride a bike. But it takes intense desire, skill, and practice to ride a unicycle. In spite of repeated failures and skinned knees at first, Jud has developed a skill worthy of a parade.

When you develop your persuasive skills, you may well feel that you are in a "parade." People will pay special attention to you. Through desire and practice, you will have learned how to lift your persuasive attempts out of the ordinary and turn them into a skill people will appreciate.

Persuasion is helping people to cooperate with you. Whether you are raising money for UNICEF, selling insurance, or trying to teach some moral value to your teenager, your persuasive skill helps people to want to do what you want them to do. Of course, not everyone will want what you want or what you can offer. But whenever agreement is possible, persuasion helps you gain a consensus. Ideally, it helps your hearers come to a decision in which both you and they win.

Persuasion, as I am using the term, is not manipulation. Manipulation aims at control, not cooperation. It results in a win—lose situation. It does not consider the good of the other party. In some circles, debasing others through manipulative techniques is actually considered chic! But the proponents of manipulation fail to point out that it eventually drives people away from the manipulator. Victims of manipulation feel resentment, distrust, and defensiveness. They will resist future attempts to force them to act against their will. They will resist being taken advantage of.

In contrast to the manipulator, the persuader seeks to enhance the self-esteem of the other party. The result is that people respond better because they are treated as responsible, self-directing individuals. This is one of the reasons why persuasion is ultimately more effective than manipulation. Semanticist S.I. Hayakawa writes:

> If it is true that everybody is trying to protect and enhance his self-concept, then your messages get through not only because you have presented them eloquently or logically, but more pertinently because of the meanings they have to the listener in the light of his interests and his self-concept. If the content of your message is seen by your listener as enhancing to his self-concept, it will be received and welcomed.[1]

Persuasive messages that enhance self-concepts require skillful effort because persuasion implies change and change is tough. Most people resist change unless they can see its resulting benefit. The process of change does not happen easily. It needs to be planned.

Yale University psychologist William McGuire suggests that the process of achieving cooperation is made more manageable when it is broken down into five steps, which can be labeled *attention, comprehension, belief, retention,* and *action.* McGuire says that the hearer must "go through each of these steps if communication is to have ultimate persuasive impact, and each depends on the occurrence of the preceding steps."[2]

As Figure 11-1 indicates, a persuasive message must not only arouse our interest, but also be clear, credible, memorable, and likely to compel action. Persuasive power is the result of mastering in your own speech each of the five steps that influence people to act in a particular way. You cannot guarantee what your hearer's response will be, but when you take these steps, you can be confident that you will have used the best means of persuasion available to you.

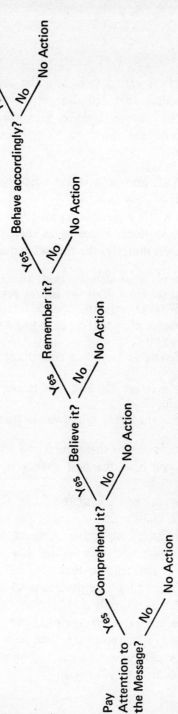

Does your listener:

Pay Attention to the Message? —Yes→ Comprehend it? —Yes→ Believe it? —Yes→ Remember it? —Yes→ Behave accordingly? —Yes→ Action

No → No Action

No → No Action

No → No Action

No → No Action

No → No Action

FIGURE 11-1. Adapted by David Myers from the writings of Yale University social psychologist William McGuire, cited in David G. Myers, *Social Psychology* (New York: McGraw-Hill, 1983), p. 275.

WIN ATTENTION

Step 1 toward persuasive action is to win the attention of your hearer. Speaking without gaining that attention is like swinging a bat without aiming at the ball. No contact is made. You never get to first base. To drive your point home, you need to make contact with your hearer's interests and attitudes.

Principle 1: Attention is won by adapting your message to the interests and attitudes of your hearers.

But how do you know the interests and attitudes of your hearers? Try to put yourself in their positions. Focus in on their points of view by asking yourself (or your hearers directly) the following questions:

1. What information is needed to best understand the person with whom I'm talking? How does the hearer perceive the subject of our conversation? What feelings are involved?
2. How is the person's life situation changing and what effect does that have on his viewpoint?
3. If I have a different opinion, how important is that difference to my hearer?
4. How does my message fit into the larger picture of my hearer's interests and values?
5. What are the relevant interests and values that we both share?

When you have the answers to these questions and are able to see things your hearer's way, you have the best chance of persuading him to see things your way.

In *The Language and Thought of the Child*, psychologist Jean Piaget writes that "a child's talk is egocentric, partly because the child speaks only about himself, but chiefly because he does not attempt to place himself at the point of view of his hearer."[3] Winning attention requires the opposite: listening so that you can get on the same wavelength with your hearer and asking questions when appropriate that show a real interest in achieving not only cooperation, but understanding.

Remember the mutual exchange principle you probably used as a child—"If you hit me, I'll hit you back!" In persuasion it works like this: "If you show me you care about understanding my position, I will listen to you and try to understand your position." So use your skills in active listening (see Chapter 4) and asking questions (see Chapter 6) to learn what your listener really thinks and feels. Whether by amplification or restatement, let it be known that you understand his position. Say:

> "I understand you to mean. . ."
> "You are saying that. . ."
> "If I take your point of view, I would. . ."

Your effort to see your hearer's viewpoint is never wasted. It provides you with valuable information about how to adapt your message to best meet objections and overcome them. It helps you to speak more directly to the mental and emotional interests of your hearers.

Keep in mind that your hearer's viewpoint is never entirely mental, but includes emotional "coloring." If you don't know the emotional coloring, you don't see the same picture. For example, if you try to sell a management training program to the president of a company, he may resist buying it, not because of the cost, but because he is afraid the program will reveal his own weaknesses. When you see the total picture, you will be able to build your message upon mutually held values and experiences. These shared features will serve as bridges of understanding and win the attention of your hearer.

IMPROVE COMPREHENSION

Step 2 toward persuasive action is to help your hearer comprehend your message. What may be clear to you may not be clear to him. He has not thought through your ideas as you have. He needs the aid of clear language, full of meaning and examples that relate to his experience.

Principle 2: Vivid language and concrete examples improve comprehension.
Have you analyzed your speech lately? So much of our language today includes fillers like "you know" and buzzwords like "functional digital capability." A governmental memorandum is reported to have included this pointless sentence:

> In the interest of integrated management flexibility, it is essential that total organizational capability be maintained so that system-

atized logistical mobility, combined with responsive policy projection, may lead to compatible management capability.

Whether the purpose is to fill space or sound authoritative, the result is
that these words become undifferentiated in the hearer's mind. One word
flows into the other without distinction, without buildup, without effect.
But our speech doesn't have to be that way! Conversation will be delight-
fully clear and persuasive when it is enhanced by language that is direct
and vigorous, aided by an imagination that can paint word pictures.

Experimental psychologists have found that in addition to clear,
vivid language, concrete examples significantly increase comprehension.
Messages that do not relate to people's experiences of frames of reference
are hard to understand and easily forgotten. Test this point after you read
the following paragraph from an experiment by John Bransford and
Marcia Johnson:

> The procedure is actually quite simple. First you arrange things into
> different groups. Of course, one pile may be sufficient depending on
> how much there is to do. ... After the procedure is completed, one
> arranges the materials into different groups again. Then they can be
> put into their proper places. Eventually they will be used once more
> and the whole cycle will then have to be repeated. However, that is a
> part of life.[4]

Now, try repeating the "simple" steps of this procedure from memory.

How did you do? Most people do not understand the procedure well
until they are told that it describes the process of washing clothes. Now
read the paragraph again and try repeating the process from memory.
Simple? Yes, because the process is familiar. Your hearer needs the same
kind of familiar references to fully comprehend your ideas.

The Bransford and Johnson experiment shows that understanding is
improved more by specific illustrations than by abstract assertions of a
general truth. Leaders know this fact and use it. When Martin Luther King,
Jr. wanted to justify to the white community the reason for his non-
violent direct action, he wrote:

> We ... are not the creators of tension. We merely bring to the sur-
> face the hidden tension that is already alive. We bring it out in the
> open, where it can be seen and dealt with.[5]

The idea that hidden tension needs to be brought out in the open in order to deal with it is a crucial point in King's argument. But it is an abstract idea. It needs to be tied to a concrete example. This is how King did it:

> Like a boil that can never be cured so long as it is covered up but must be opened with all its ugliness to the natural medicines of air and light, injustice must be exposed, with all the tension its exposure creates, to the light of human conscience and the air of national opinion before it can be cured.[6]

Whether you are speaking to a large segment of society or to one or two listeners, each person must understand your words before he can act on them. To increase the clarity of your presentation, ask yourself these questions:

> Is my speech clear and free from jargon?
> Does my main idea make sense to my hearer?
> Have I used vivid language and concrete examples to improve comprehension?

GENERATE BELIEF

Step 3 toward persuasive action is to generate belief in your message. Belief is the psychological "yes" to what you are saying. Without that "yes," you will not get the positive response you want.

How do you get people to the "yes"? The answer depends on many factors, including your present and past actions, your personality, social status, fairness, objectivity, and nonverbal cues (appearance, voice, fluency, rate of speech, physical mannerisms). However, there are two overriding factors in generating belief: showing enthusiasm about your message and providing evidence to support your position.

Principle 3: Belief is generated by enthusiasm and evidence.
Enthusiasm tells your hearer that you believe what you are saying. You do not need to be eloquent, or clever, or sensational, or famous; you *must* believe what you say and show that you do. When you express enthusiasm

for your message, you convey a special charismatic quality that is almost irresistible to an audience. Enthusiasm compels belief.

The secret power of enthusiasm lies in the fact that it intrigues people. Immediately they wonder why you are so turned on about your idea. Like trying to solve a mystery, they will look for clues. They'll listen for some meaning they may have missed. When this happens, you have created a persuasive situation because as the philosopher Blaise Pascal remarked, "People are usually more convinced by reasons they discover themselves than by those found by others."[7] Your enthusiasm gets the listener hot on the trail to find reasons for your point of view.

Evidence is the second major factor in the process of generating belief. Evidence is information that can be verified. For example:

> "If we project a ten percent growth rate over the next five years, you can see that the demand for our product will exceed our present manufacturing capabilities."
>
> "You say you need to staple fifty pages at a time. Watch how this machine handles that job."
>
> "I can understand your hesitancy about this investment. John Campanero, who referred me to you, felt the same way at first. However, after three weeks on this program he wrote this letter to me, which you may read."

To be convincing your evidence must be relevant, reliable, and available. The best way to determine if the evidence you select will convince your hearer is to ask yourself the following questions, keeping your hearer's viewpoint in mind:

1. Does this information help the listener understand my solution to the problem? (Relevance)
2. Will the listener consider this information to be trustworthy? Will he trust the original source or the person who gathered the data? (Reliability)
3. Can my listener check the truth of my data if he wants to? (Availability)

Convincing evidence answers the questions or objections your hearer might have and prepares him to believe you. Your purpose is not to prove you are right, but that he is right in acting on your idea.

INCREASE RETENTION

Step 4 toward persuasive action is to ensure the retention of your message. If your hearer does not remember what you've said, all your previous steps toward persuasive action will have been wasted. In order to act, your hearer must be able to recall what you persuaded him to do.

Studies show that we remember information better if it is presented repeatedly and spaced over a period of time. Experimental psychologist Lynn Hasher found that repeated information is more credible than a single exposure to the information. Other experiments show that repeated presentations of a stimulus tend to increase people's liking of it. What is more credible and better liked will be remembered longer.

Principle 4: Spaced repetition increases retention.

Capitalize on the power of spaced repetition. Ask yourself: "What do I most want people to remember in my presentation? How can I rephrase the controlling ideas to make them unforgettable?" Sometimes you can capture the key idea in a single sentence, or even in a single word repeated throughout your message. Martin Luther King, Jr. achieved dramatic results by using this principle in his "I have a dream" speech.

In some cases you may want your listener not necessarily to concentrate on the facts you present, but rather to remember his favorable reactions to these facts. To do this you can repeat a question throughout your speech or build up to it at the end of your presentation. In the 1980 presidential campaign debate between Jimmy Carter and Ronald Reagan, Reagan produced an unforgettable effect in the listener's mind, not by repeating the facts he presented, but by emphasizing their effect with this rhetorical question: "Are you better off today than you were four years ago?" That question helped him win the debate and the election. Thus, your goal may not necessarily be to repeat facts, but to help your listener remember his positive reactions to your presentation.

If your situation allows it, ask your hearer to tell you what each point means to him. This helps him to actively process your ideas mentally. A parent can save a great deal of hassle simply by asking his child: "Cindy, what did I ask you to do?" A manager might say: "After I finish this report, I'm going to ask you what you feel are the key points we need to discuss and act on." If your hearer can repeat your ideas or state his reactions to your ideas, he can remember them.

ASK FOR ACTION

The fifth and final step in persuasion is to ask for action. You may present interesting, clear, credible, and memorable ideas, but if your hearer doesn't act on them, you have not been persuasive. Action is the end product of persuasion.

What is your aim when you attempt to persuade someone? What action do you want your listener to take? Perhaps you want your listener to:

Give you a check for the product you sell.
Implement a behavioral change,
Make a contribution to a charity.
Give you a pay raise or promotion.

Whatever it is, you must be sure to *ask* for the action you want.

Principle 5: To get action, ask for it.

When our attempts at persuasion fail, it is often because we are hesitant to ask another person to do something. We assume that our hearer should "get the message" and initiate his own action on the force of our ideas. But usually it doesn't work that way. Our hearers are constantly bombarded with ideas. One study estimates that the average person's brain handles about 10,000 ideas a day. Relatively few of these ideas are acted upon. To get action, we need to ask for it.

Make your request for action specific and clear. For example:

"If you would like to take advantage of this offer, please call me before five today at my office."

"I would like to take you out for dinner Friday evening. May I call for you at seven?"

"Your contribution can help needy children just like Jennifer. I ask you to make out a check to the Crippled Children's Fund and give it to Mrs. Johnson before you leave tonight."

Seeking immediate reaction generally is best. Expert salesmen try to get a check or signature immediately after their presentation—not a week or two later. The longer the lapse time, the less appeal your idea is likely to have. Strike while the idea is hot.

If you feel frustrated because you have not been getting the cooperation that you need, review these five principles of persuasion. You may be overlooking one of them. Revising your message according to these basic techniques usually can save the day. Just remember:

1. Attention is won by adapting your message to the interests and attitudes of your hearer.
2. Vivid language and concrete examples improve comprehension.
3. Belief is generated by enthusiasm and convincing evidence.
4. Spaced repetition increases retention.
5. To get action, ask for it.

After you achieve initial success with your persuasive skills, keep going. Raise your self-expectation level a few more degrees, refine your presentation in reference to each of the five principles, and try again. You will gain confidence as you do. You will be eager for the next "parade" in which people pay special attention to you.

After winning attention in his first parade, my son now is eager to try his skills again—on a six-foot unicycle!

ACTION STEPS
FOR WINNING SELF-DIRECTION

1. Focus your attention on one person whom you find to be very persuasive and then answer these questions: Why do you find him persuasive? How many of the five steps to persuasion does he employ? How does he use each step? (e.g.: How does he win your attention? How does he help you understand? etc.)

2. Now think about some action you want another person to take. For example, you may want your teenager in the house by 11:00 P.M. weeknights or you may want your boss to give you a raise. Develop your appeal for cooperation by writing your thoughts in answer to these questions:

How can I win the attention of my listener?
How can I increase his comprehension of what I want him to do?
How can I help him believe that he is right in cooperating with me?
How can I make my ideas, or his favorable reactions to my ideas, unforgettable?
How can I obtain the action I want?

12

Enjoy success

From the fruit of his lips a man enjoys good things.[1]

KING SOLOMON

Personal success—what does it mean to you? What brings you the most enjoyment? Your answers may be different from the answers of your friends or family. But however you define success, the good things you enjoy are more abundant when you communicate at your highest level.

PEAK COMMUNICATION EXPERIENCES

While reading this book and working toward your own communication goals, you likely have increased your skills and reached new levels of achievement. You are on your way to becoming a "peak communicator."

As you read this section, which reviews the twelve major communication goals set forth in this book, visualize yourself achieving each of these goals; think of yourself as a peak communicator.

1. You Set Goals to Win.   As a peak communicator, you are determined to be a winner. You enter every conversation with your mind set on overcoming the boulders of resistance in your way, such as misunderstand-

173

ing, wrong judgments, and inattentiveness. Sometimes you fail. But when you fail, you attempt to learn why. You reexamine your goals for clarity and then dare to move forward again to reach them. You know that the only way to play the communication game is to play to win. For this reason, you develop game plans. You practice strategies that work. You refine your goals. Not the least of your joys is the fact that when you win the communication game, you help your partner in communication to win, too!

2. You Become All You Can Be.   As a peak communicator, you know that you will never reach your highest potential unless you analyze your weaknesses and build upon your strengths. So you develop realistic estimates of who you are and who you want to become. You don't waste time trying to defend past mistakes. You intend to get yourself right so your words come out right. This goal introduces a positive dynamic in your dialogues—less defensiveness, more openness, greater understanding.

3. You Eliminate Negative Communication Habits.   As a peak communicator, *you* determine your level of communication. Your words, attitudes, goals, strategies, and personal commitments are all matters of your choice. Consequently, you can effectively eliminate the obnoxious habits that so easily creep into conversations and damage them.

4. You Listen Deeply.   As a peak communicator, you take time for deep listening. You plumb the depths of your partner's mind and heart. You ask questions and you listen carefully to the answers—not just to the words, but to the feelings behind the words. Instead of evaluating each answer and thereby prompting your partner to withdraw, you assist your partner in saying what he really wants to say. Sometimes you let certain remarks drift into oblivion because they are unimportant; but you respond to other remarks that, although they may seem inconsequential, actually point to significant thoughts and feelings buried in some hidden chamber of the mind. As a peak communicator, you seek to draw out the best and leave the rest. Your payoff is the enjoyment of the best that human relationships can offer.

5. You Know How Communication Works.   As a peak communicator, you study the effects of your words. Like a competent doctor, you use more than one diagnostic tool or point of view to locate a problem and solve it. Feedback helps you fine-tune what you say and correctly interpret what you hear. As a peak communicator, you stand in stark contrast to the poor soul who doesn't know he's boring, or talking too loud, or completely missing the point. You quickly sense when something goes wrong with the communication process. You know how to make adjustments to increase understanding.

6. You Win People's Attention. As a peak communicator, you find people fascinating. You learn to ask questions that bring out the depth of character and interesting history of your communication partners. You assume the best about your partners and help them to express their best. Consequently, when you speak, your partners listen. As a peak communicator, you can speak convincingly on a wide range of topics of interest to you because you have taken the time to work through your thoughts and discover your true feelings. You are neither belligerent nor defensive about your views because you feel reasonably secure about stating what you think, even to a disagreeing audience. But you also maintain an openness to alternatives and are able to change your mind when an alternative to your view is superior. You enjoy dialogue. You are delightful to hear.

7. You Have the Courage to Say No. As a peak communicator, you know when to say yes and when to say no. Whenever it is appropriate, you say yes to others because, at heart, you are a positive person. The primary factor that determines how you respond is not what other people think, but what *you* think in reference to your own values. Thus, you have an inner standard for saying yes or no. If your answer is no, it is firm, but not antagonistic. It doesn't invite retaliation and it doesn't open the door to nagging. You are clear and direct, so that no second-guessing of your intention is required. You are authentic.

8. You Respect Children. As a peak communicator, you respect children. Remembering your own childhood, you talk with children the way you wanted adults to talk with you. You enjoy listening to children, answering their questions, and sensing how mysterious and intriguing the world must look to them. Children, in turn, respond with respect. They feel encouraged to share their real thoughts. Knowing they are understood, they feel good about themselves. They are then most open to instruction and the transfer of significant values.

9. You Achieve Intimacy. As a peak communicator, you care as much about people close to you as you do about yourself. You know that intimacy begins with a desire for the well-being of your family and friends, that mere words cannot substitute for empathy and compassion. Self-disclosure is always balanced with discretion. You know the risk involved in creating closeness, but you also know the potential for joy and mutual fulfillment. You know that caring commitments minimize the chances of alienation. Thus, you commit yourself to those close to you, striving never to betray a confidence or break an agreement. Trust, freedom to be yourself, readiness to share what you think and feel without fear—these ingredients in your communication yield self-discovery and a sense of interpersonal fulfillment.

10. You Dissolve Discord. As a peak communicator, you are not afraid of conflict. You don't suppress or ignore tensions, but you do realize the damage relentless tension can do to a relationship. When you encounter misunderstanding and polarization, you do your best to resolve the conflict by following a clear plan: (1) you define the problem; (2) you look for areas of agreement; (3) you seek to understand the feelings; and (4) you calmly state what you think. Your conversations are filled with words and phrases like "we . . . us . . . our . . . what are you thinking? . . . how do you feel about the level of our communication? . . . how can we solve the problem? . . . let's consider . . . , negotiate . . . , resolve."

11. You Gain Cooperation. As a peak communicator, you persuade people to cooperate with you. Manipulation, deceit, high-pressure tactics—these are foreign to your style and values. Rather, you win attention by tuning in to the other person's wavelength. You use vivid and concrete examples to make sure your listener comprehends what you are saying. You are enthusiastic because you believe cooperation will be mutually beneficial. You give evidence showing the value of your point of view. The result is that you are highly credible. When you ask for action, you usually get it.

12. You Enjoy Success. As a peak communicator, you enjoy a fruitful life. Goal setting and winning strategies have become a part of your daily experience. Consequently, when you talk with your conversational partner, there is a meeting of minds and a blending of hearts. Through first-hand experience you know the truth of the assertion made in Chapter 1: nothing is more essential to success in any area of your life than the ability to communicate well. Surely, as the proverb says, "From the fruit of his lips a man enjoys good things."

POSITIVE ADDICTION

Why do some people endure the sweat, hard work, and occasional pain of running three, five, or ten miles a day? Psychiatrist William Glasser found that when a jogger reaches a certain level of fitness, when he feels a physical, mental, and emotional exuberance as a result of his effort, he experiences "positive addiction." He keeps going because he knows the benefits outweigh the discomforts.

Positive addiction will also keep you going in your effort to gain a higher level of communication "fitness." At first, like a beginning jogger, you may experience fatigue and a desire to give up. But if you keep setting *specific, measurable, affirmative, realistic, time-constricted* (SMART) goals and working on practical strategies for reaching them, your conversations gradually will become easier—more natural and less tense, freer and less fearful. It is this fresh sense of increase, this thrilling experience of greater fulfillment, that can create positive addiction in your own efforts to improve your communication.

Never give up! When you exercise your peak communication skills consistently, you enhance the bond of understanding between you and another and maintain the flow of revitalizing ideas. You experience that special sort of pleasure of functioning in top form. You take comfort in the fact that you have learned how to handle even obnoxious people with maximum skill. Such skills are exhilarating. Once you experience them, you will not be satisfied with anything less than your best. You will find peak communication to be positvely addicting.

THE PRESENT MOMENT

When you approach the end of your life, how do you think you will evaluate your significant personal relationships? What will stand out in your memory as the most happy moments? What experiences will you wish you could have changed? Will you have done all you could to achieve satisfying, enriching communication in the home, among friends, and at work?

Unfortunately, many people cheat themselves out of the most precious moments of life. They drift from one misunderstanding and heartbreak to another without knowing they could make it better, without a plan of action for solving their problems. They feel imprisoned by failure. But whatever has occurred in the past is history! It is gone and cannot be relived. When this obvious fact is forgotten, we waste tremendous amounts of energy trying to undo what has been done, to take back words that have already been said. Certainly we must learn from past failures or we are doomed to repeat them. But our primary attention ought to be directed toward the future and the management of present tasks.

The present moment is manageable! If I had to repair all my past and future mistakes in one conversation, then I would give up in despair. But if I correct misunderstanding in the present, then there is hope for today—and tomorrow.

Perhaps you have come to a fork in the road in terms of your relationships with your family, friends, or business associates—a time for choosing how you will relate to them. Will you choose counterproductive patterns of communication or set out on the path that leads to peak experiences in dialogue—the enjoyment of "the fruit of your lips"? Your choice will make all the difference.

The Successful Communicator's Creed

I believe family, friends, and business associates are worth the effort required for successful communication. Although I can't control how they respond to me, I can control how I respond to them. I can admit my mistakes and correct them. I can change even long-standing habits in communication by understanding how communication works, by setting worthwhile goals for my interpersonal relationships, and by committing myself to developing my conversational skills.

Children and adults listen to me because I actively listen to them and respect them. Friends share their thoughts and feelings openly with me because they know I have learned how to be a true friend.

When conflicts arise, I follow a clear plan for resolving them. I know how to persuade people to cooperate with me. I enjoy success in my interpersonal relationships because I have learned the art of talking so that people will listen.

ACTION STEPS
FOR WINNING SELF-DIRECTION

To maintain your communication skills and to increase your level of expertise, use the following questions as a stimulus to your development. Update your answers every few months.

1. *What changes do you still need to make?* To help you answer this question, you may want to retake the Self-Evaluation in the first chapter. Examine the areas in which you feel you need more work and commit yourself to your plan for improvement.

2. *How will you monitor your progress?* Keep a journal to note your progress. Write down significant exchanges verbatim as you remember them and examine them for weaknesses and strengths. Perhaps you could ask a friend to help you monitor your progress.

3. *How will you know when you have met a goal?* Set *specific, measurable, affirmative, realistic, time-constricted* (SMART) goals. Specify the communication behavior you want and set deadlines. For example, "By _____, I will _____."

4. *How will you reward yourself when you achieve a goal?* The reward doesn't need to be costly. Anything will do that visibly points to your success. For example, take your best friend out for lunch, go to the theater, buy your favorite record, or celebrate with a party.

5. *What will you do when you fail to achieve a goal?* Never give up. When you try and fail, make adjustments and try again.

6. *How will you motivate yourself to keep going toward your communication goals?* Make certain that your goals are clear and that they refer to actions that *you* can control. Visualize the benefits of reaching your goals. Read the Successful Communicator's Creed often. Believe you can achieve each of your clearly defined, worthwhile, personal communication goals.

FEEDBACK

What success have you enjoyed as a result of reaching your communication goals? What communication problems seem to resist your attempts to solve them? I would like to hear from you and respond to your feedback either directly by mail or indirectly in my next book, *The Art of Talking So Teenagers Listen.* Of course, all names will be kept confidential.

I believe personal encouragement and guidance can help you to master the skills and develop the goals you have read about in this book. If either you or your firm would like to receive information on Interpersonal Communication Seminars in your area, please write to me:

Dr. Paul Swets
256 Greenbrier Dr.
Palm Springs, FL 33461

Notes

CHAPTER ONE

1. Norman Vincent Peale, *You Can If You Think You Can* (New York: Fawcett Crest, 1974), p. 12.

CHAPTER TWO

1. Ralph Waldo Emerson, quoted in Michael J. Mahoney, *Self Change: Strategies for Solving Personal Problems* (New York: Norton, 1979), p. 13.

2. Ralph Waldo Emerson.

3. Thomas A. Harris, *I'm OK – You're OK* (New York: Harper & Row, 1969), p. 113.

4. Mark Twain, quoted in Cecil Osborne, *Release from Fear and Anxiety* (New York: Pillar, 1977), p. 11.

5. John B. Watson, *Behaviorism* (New York: Norton, 1924), p. 8.

6. Wendell Johnson, *Your Most Enchanted Listener* (New York: Harper & Row, 1956), p. 88.

7. John McKay, quoted in James Dobson, *Hide or Seek* (Old Tappan, N.J.: Revell, 1974), p. 7.

8. Paul Tournier, *To Understand Each Other* (Atlanta, GA.: John Knox Press, 1962), p. 30.

CHAPTER THREE

1. Norman Cousins, *Human Options* (New York: Norton, 1981), pp. 46, 67.

CHAPTER FOUR

1. Seneca, quoted in Taylor Caldwell, *The Listener* (New York: Bantam, 1960), p. vi.

2. Originally appeared in the Pennsylvania Law Enforcement Journal.

3. "Archie Bunker," quoted in Thomas Banville, *How to Be Heard* (Chicago: Nelson-Hall, 1978), p. 67.

4. William Shakespeare, quoted in Earl Koile, *Listening as a Way of Becoming* (Waco, Tex.: Regency, 1977), p. 116.

5. Wendell Johnson, *Your Most Enchanted Listener* (New York: Harper & Row, 1956), p. 21.

6. Joseph T. Bayly, *The Last Thing We Talk About* (Elgin, Illinois: D.C. Cook, 1969), pp. 40-41.

CHAPTER FIVE

1. Mark Twain, quoted in *Write Better, Speak Better* (New York: Reader's Digest Association, 1977), p. 386.

2. John Gottman, *A Couple's Guide to Communication* (Champaign, Ill.: Research Press, 1977), p. xix.

3. Carl Rogers, "Communication: Its Blocking and Facilitation," *ETC: A Review of General Semantics* 9, no. 2; copyright 1952 by the International Society for General Semantics.

4. Ibid.

5. Mark Twain, "Buck Fanshaw's Funeral," in *The Complete Short Stories of Mark Twain*, Charles Neider, ed. (New York: Doubleday, 1957), p. 73.

CHAPTER SIX

1. Wendell Johnson, *Your Most Enchanted Listener* (New York: Harper & Row, 1956), p. 193.

2. *Palm Beach Post,* March 5, 1979, p. C-3.

3. Harry Lorayne and Jerry Lucas, *The Memory Book* (Briarcliff Manor, New York: Stein & Day, 1974), pp. 67-68.

CHAPTER SEVEN

1. John Holt, *How Children Fail* (New York: Delta, 1964), p. 34.

2. Aaron Hass, *Teenage Sexuality—A Survey of Teenage Sexual Behavior* (New York: Macmillan, 1981), quoted in *Palm Beach Post,* January 14, 1980, p. A-14.

3. Abraham Maslow, *Toward a Psychology of Being* (New York: Van Nostrand Reinhold, 1968), p. 106.

4. Blaise Pascal, *Pensees: Thoughts on Religion and Other Subjects,* translated by W.F. Trotter (New York: Washington Square Press, 1965), p. 137.

CHAPTER EIGHT

1. Haim G. Ginott, *Between Parent and Child* (New York: Macmillan, 1965), p. 21.

2. W. Livingston Larned, quoted in Dale Carnegie, *How to Win Friends and Influence People* (New York: Pocket Books, 1940), pp. 239-40.

3. S. I. Hayakawa, *Symbol, Status, and Personality* (New York: Harcourt, Brace & World, 1963), p. 47.

4. Eric Fromm, *The Art of Loving* (New York: Harper & Row, 1956), p. 23.

5. Bruce Narramore, *Help, I'm a Parent* (Grand Rapids, Mich.: Zondervan, 1972), p. 41.

6. Benjamin Spock, quoted in *Redbook's Parent and Child,* (New York: Redbook, 1976), p. 10.

7. Alice Ginott, "How to Drive Your Children Sane," *Ladies Home Journal,* August 1977, p. 48.

8. Plato, *The Republic,* trans. Francis M. Cornford (New York: Oxford University Press, 1941), Book II, p. 69.

9. Urie Bronfenbrenner, *Two Worlds of Childhood: The US and USSR* (New York: Russell Sage Foundation, 1970), pp. 102-3.

10. Jesse Jackson, quoted in *Time*, July 10, 1978, p. 46.

CHAPTER NINE

1. Dag Hammarskjöld, *Markings* (New York: Knopf, 1964), p. 40.

CHAPTER TEN

1. Thomas Gordon, *Leader Effectiveness Training* (New York: Wyden, 1979), pp. 146-47.

2. S. I. Hayakawa, *Symbol, Status, and Personality* (New York: Harcourt, Brace and World, 1963), pp. 34-35.

3. Adapted from drawings by Malik, reproduced by permission of the National Peace Academy, 110 Maryland Ave., N.E., Washington, D.C. 20002.

CHAPTER ELEVEN

1. S. I. Hayakawa, *Symbol, Status, and Personality* (New York: Harcourt, Brace & World, 1963), p. 45-46.

2. William J. McGuire in *Handbook of Social Psychology*, ed. Gardner Lindsey and Elliot Aronson (Reading, Mass.: Addison-Wesley, 1967), 3:173.

3. Jean Piaget, *The Language and Thought of the Child* (Atlantic Highlands, N.J.: Humanities Press, 1962), p. 6.

4. John Bransford and Marcia Johnson, "Consideration of Some Problems of Comprehension," in *Visual Information Processing*, ed. W. G. Chase (New York: Academic Press, 1973).

5. Martin Luther King, Jr., *Why We Can't Wait* (New York: Harper & Row, 1963), p. 88.

6. Ibid.

7. Blaise Pascal, quoted in Gerard I. Nierenberg and Henry H. Calero, *Meta-Talk: Guide to Hidden Meanings in Conversations* (New York: Simon & Schuster, 1973), p. 77.

CHAPTER TWELVE

1. Proverbs 13:2. Taken from the *Holy Bible: New International Version*, copyright 1978 by the New York International Bible Society.

Index